SPINAbilities

A Young Person's Guide
To Spina Bifida

Edited by Marlene Lutkenhoff, R.N., M.S.N.,
and Sonya G. Oppenheimer, M.D.

Woodbine House 1997

Illustrations: Eric Lutkenhoff

Library of Congress Cataloging-in-Publication Data

SPINAbilities : a young person's guide to spina bifida / edited by Marlene Lutkenhoff, Sonya G. Oppenheimer.

   p. cm.

  Includes index.

  Summary: A guide to coping with the medical, self-care, and emotional issues of spina bifida, with an emphasis on becoming as independent as possible.

  ISBN 0-933149-86-7 (paper)

  1. Spina bifida—Juvenile literature. 2. Spina bifida—Psychological aspects—Juvenile literature. 3. Physically handicapped teenagers—Juvenile literature. [1. Spina bifida. 2. Physically handicapped.] I. Lutkenhoff, Marlene. II. Oppenheimer, Sonya.

RJ496.S74S695 1996   96-42056

616.8'3—dc20   CIP

                            AC

Manufactured in the United States of America

10 9 8 7 6 5 4 3 2 1

Table of Contents

Foreword v

PART ONE: Your Health and Personal Care

Chapter 1: Spina Who? 3
(What Spina Bifida Is and How It Affects Me)
Marlene Lutkenhoff, R.N., M.S.N.

Chapter 2: Taking Care of Business 11
(Self Care)
Linda Custis-Allen, M.S., OTR/L

Chapter 3: Caring for Your Largest Organ 21
(Skin Care)
Marlene Lutkenhoff, R.N., M.S.N.

Chapter 4: Solid Waste 27
(The Bowels)
Roberta Hills, R.N., M.S.

Chapter 5: Waterworks 35
(Care of Your Urinary Tract)
Nan Tobias, M.S.N., R.N., CS, P.N.P.

Chapter 6: Walking & Wheeling 43
(Mobility Issues)
Catherine Lowe, M.S., P.T.

PART TWO: Relationships

Chapter 7: Great Expectations 57
(Relationships and Developing Independence)
Sharon Sellet, B.S.

Chapter 8: Family Matters 63
Sharon Sellet, B.S.

Chapter 9: Intimate Details 71
(Sexuality Issues)
Marlene Lutkenhoff, R.N., M.S.N.

PART THREE: Growing Up

Chapter 10: Tools & Techniques 81
(for School and Beyond)
Sharon Sellet, B.S.

Chapter 11: Payday 95
(Career Planning)
Linda Custis-Allen, M.S., OTR/L

PART FOUR: Healthy Practices

Chapter 12: Healthy Practices 113
Marlene Lutkenhoff, R.N., M.S.N.

Chapter 13: Basic Training 123
(Fitness, Exercise, and Sports)
Catherine Lowe, M.S., P.T.

Contributors 133

Index 135

Foreword

Spina bifida has been known since early times. Until recently, however, doctors did not know how to treat it effectively. Sadly, many lives were cut short due to a lack of medical technology and knowledge.

Today, technology and knowledge have greatly improved. We now know that many doctors and other professionals must team together to provide the best treatment for young people with spina bifida. When several professionals from different fields (disciplines) team together, they are called a multidisciplinary team.

In 1964, one of the first multidisciplinary teams was formed at the University Affiliated Cincinnati Center for Developmental Disorders. At that time, the primary concern of parents and physicians was "will the baby born with spina bifida survive?" Today, our concerns focus on helping people with spina bifida live a full and active life. As we move into the twenty-first century, those "babies" we knew in the '60s and '70s are adults. Some of them have had successful careers, have married, and have had children. Others have not done as well and are struggling with unemployment and problems with their health and medical insurance. Since our focus has changed from survival to full participation in the community, our hope is that the adults of the future will be more successful in achieving their dreams.

Our team worries that many professionals pay a great deal of attention to the young child with spina bifida, but sometimes ignore the issues of adolescence and young adulthood. We hope that this book can help to improve that situation.

We hope that it will give you some answers to the questions you have about yourself and your future. Remember, no one has all the answers, but this book will hopefully give you some directions that will help you find the answers.

Sonya Oppenheimer, M.D.
Marlene Lutkenhoff, R.N., M.S.N.

PART ONE

Your

Health

and

Personal

Care

(1)

SPINA Who?

(What Spina Bifida Is And How It Affects Me)

Marlene Lutkenhoff, R.N., M.S.N.

What?

If you have spina bifida, something went wrong with the way your spinal cord formed before birth. Usually, the spinal cord is a closed tube made up of nerves. These nerves allow messages to travel from your brain to the nerves in your muscles, telling them to move. These nerves also carry messages that allow you to feel. When a baby is born with spina bifida, the tube is not closed. Because of this, the backbone and skin surrounding the spinal cord are also not closed. The baby is born with an opening in his back, and messages have trouble getting through to his nerves. When nerves cannot communicate properly with the brain, *paralysis* (inability to move and feel) result.

Which nerves are affected depend on where the opening on the back is. The higher the opening is on the back, the more nerves are affected and the more paralysis there is. That is why some people with spina bifida walk with little or no bracing and others use a wheelchair.

Why?

That's a good question that we are still trying to answer. But we do know that it is no one's fault when a child is born with spina bifida.

A vitamin B (folic acid) may play a part. Folic acid is believed to help make the spinal tube close. If there is not enough folic acid in the mother, the baby's spinal tube may not close properly. This is one explanation that has not been totally proved.

A known fact is that spina bifida can be caused by genetic factors. This means that it occurs in some families more than others. There is one medication some mothers take to prevent seizures, Valproic Acid, that is known to cause spina bifida. There may be many other causes that are still unknown.

When?

Spina bifida occurs very early in pregnancy, within the first 28 days of prenatal life. That's why it's called a birth defect. It's different from a spinal cord injury that occurs later in life—say, from a car accident or sports injury. Although someone with a spinal cord injury also has difficulties with his legs, bladder, and bowel, he will not get hydrocephalus and need a shunt. His leg muscles may be well-developed because he used to walk without problems. You might know or have heard of famous people who have been injured in this way.

This is the way one young man with spina bifida responded to the question "What is the biggest way spina bifida affects your life?"

"It affects many functionings, but probably the biggest way is that simply knowing and performing simple tasks takes twice as long. With that, also knowing I will have spina bifida the rest of my life. That is very hard to face; however, I look to other means for strength." —J.M.P.

Who?

Any parent can have a child born with spina bifida. In the United States, 1 out of 1,000 babies is affected with spina bifida. There are a few more girls than boys born with this disability. It occurs less in Afro-American families than in white families.

Did You Know?

Spina bifida means split or open spine. Another name for spina bifida is *myelomeningocele* (my-low-meh-nin-go-seal).

Commonly Affected Areas

People with spina bifida are not necessarily sick. But they may have problems with certain body systems. The systems most affected are the nervous system (brain and spine), the urinary system (bladder and bowel), and the orthopedic system (bones and joints).

BRAIN AND SPINE

Hydrocephalus occurs when spinal fluid, which nourishes the nervous system inside the brain, cannot get out. Instead of going out and down the spinal cord, it builds up inside the brain. Luckily, we can take care of this problem by putting a *shunt* (tube) inside the brain to help drain the fluid.

Shunt. The shunt usually takes the fluid from the brain to an open area around the stomach. The fluid then goes back into the blood like it is supposed to. People cannot tell you have a shunt by looking at you. It is inside your body. Not all people with spina bifida have hydrocephalus and a shunt, but 95 percent do.

Sometimes a shunt stops working because it comes apart, gets plugged up, is too short, or just falls apart. If that happens, a neurosurgeon, a surgeon who operates on the brain and spinal cord, will operate and fix what is wrong.

Some common signs the shunt isn't working are:

- ◎ Vomiting
- ◎ Headaches
- ◎ Vision problems
  (cross-eyed, double vision)
- ◎ More tired than usual
- ◎ Easily upset
- ◎ Don't feel right.

The shunt can stop working at any time, even if you are fully grown. If you are having problems, don't ignore these symptoms. Call your family doctor or your neurosurgeon. An operation may be necessary to fix the shunt. If you need a shunt, without the operation your symptoms may get worse, and could lead to death. If you respond quickly to warning signs, the shunt can be easily repaired or replaced.

Tethered Cord

Tethered cord means scar tissue that forms following back surgery. This scar tissue can attach itself to the spinal cord and to nearby bone, causing the spinal cord to be pulled on, sort of like a tug of war. Often, this happens during periods of growth. Symptoms of a tethered cord are:

◎ Back pain
◎ More difficulty walking
◎ Scoliosis—curvature of the spine
◎ Changes in bowel or bladder function;
   increased accidents
◎ Changes in the way you walk

You should see your family doctor or a neurosurgeon if you have these symptoms. X-rays and lab tests will be necessary to help the doctor decide what is wrong. An operation may be necessary to remove the scar tissue. Although all people with spina bifida are at risk for tethered cord, only some develop problems that require surgery.

Arnold Chiari

Almost all individuals with spina bifida have what is known as *Arnold Chiari.* This is a brain abnormality named after the two scientists who discovered it. Arnold Chiari refers to a physical problem within the brain. It means that part of the lower brain has slipped down into the top part of the spinal canal. This is why hydrocephalus develops.

Most people never have problems from Arnold Chiari once a shunt is in place, but a few do. Some symptoms of Arnold Chiari problems may include swallowing difficulties, breathing problems, and/or arm weakness. Sometimes there is pain at the back of the neck. A neurosurgeon may order an MRI (discussed below), and an operation may be needed.

Hydromyelia and Syringomyelia

Hydromyelia refers to a cavity or space that has cerebral-spinal fluid within it. When that cavity is within the spinal cord, it is called *syringomyelia.* The space or cavity is called a *syrinx.* Signs of a syrinx are:
◎ Weak or jerky arms
◎ More difficulty with walking
◎ Scoliosis

The neurosurgeon will sometimes put a permanent shunt (tube) into the cavity to drain the fluid away. Hydromyelia and syringomyelia are not that common, but can occur at any time.

Tests to Look at the Brain and Spinal Cord

Although some of these tests are done routinely, the frequency of tests varies depending on your age and development of certain symptoms.

CT Scan. A CT scan is a type of X-ray that takes pictures of cross sections of the brain. The pictures show up on a TV screen. Sometimes medicine is given through a vein so that the pictures will show up clearly. The test is not painful.

MRI. An MRI uses a magnet, radio waves, and a computer to take pictures of the inside of the brain and spinal cord. Sometimes medicine is given through a vein to help the pictures on the TV screen show up clearly. Although the MRI machine makes noises while it is taking the pictures, having an MRI does not hurt.

BLADDER AND BOWEL

Bladder

Almost all people with spina bifida have problems with their *bladder*—the organ that stores urine. The nerves that control the bladder are some of the nerves that were damaged before you were born. This means you may have trouble getting all the urine out of your bladder or it may drip out constantly. That is why many people with spina bifida *catheterize* themselves (insert a tube into the bladder to drain the urine).

It is important that a doctor see you regularly to be sure your kidneys are doing okay. Urine held in the bladder can back up to the kidneys and cause damage. Once damage occurs, it cannot be fixed. Kidney damage can occur without you knowing it, so there are tests to help the doctor know what is happening inside. The doctor may take your blood pressure because high blood pressure can mean kidney problems. High blood pressure can occur for other reasons, too.

Because bladder problems are so common, Chapter 5 takes a closer look at the subject.

Bowel

Almost all people with spina bifida have problems with bowel control. The bowel is an organ that stores waste material. When nerves that control the bowel do not function as they should, it is difficult to feel when you need to have a bowel movement. It is also difficult to have enough muscle control to wait until you are on the toilet to have a bowel movement. That is why many people with spina bifida use digital stimulation, suppositories, and enemas to help them manage their bowels.

See Chapter 4 for more information.

BONES AND JOINTS

Less Sensation and Movement

How much sensation (feeling) and movement you have in your lower legs depends a lot on where that open area on your back was. If the open area was fairly high on your back, you may have little or no movement or sensation in your legs. The lower the area was, generally, the more movement and sensation you have. This is because different muscles are controlled by nerves that connect to the spinal cord at different locations. Generally, the higher the open area was, the more nerves involved.

Remember that nerves carry messages from the brain to where they need to go. If the messages can't get through, movement can't occur. For example, if your open area was high, the nerves that control hip movement are affected. If your open area was very low on your back, the nerves that control your ankles and feet will be affected. Therefore, people with spina bifida usually use braces, crutches, walkers, and wheelchairs to help them get around.

Sometimes surgery is necessary to help keep bones in the best position for walking. You may need a physical therapist to help you learn to use your body in the best way possible. Although it is not easy to transfer from a wheelchair to a car and back again, many people can learn to do it with the help of a therapist. You may want to read these two chapters for more information: *Taking Care of Business* (2) and *Walking & Wheeling* (6).

Scoliosis

Many people with spina bifida develop scoliosis, or a curved backbone. This is because of muscle imbalance resulting from failure of the spinal cord to form normally. Scoliosis can develop at any age, but is more likely to occur during periods of rapid growth.

A curved backbone can cause a variety of problems, such as poor sitting balance. This, in turn, can lead to pressure sores on the butt. Severe scoliosis can affect the ability of the lungs to fully expand, possibly leading to breathing problems. Bracing and/or surgery is sometimes needed to prevent scoliosis from getting worse.

Fractures

People with spina bifida have a higher risk of breaking bones (fractures). This is because you may not feel some parts of your body, and because the bones in your legs may be weaker from not standing or using them. To reduce the chance of a fracture, be sure to warm up properly before exercising or taking part in strenuous activities. Read Chapter 13 for more tips about fitness and exercise.

Signs of a possible fracture are:

- ◎ Swelling
- ◎ Heat or redness
- ◎ Pain—You may not feel pain if the fracture occurs in an area where you have little or no sensation.

If you suspect a fracture, call your general physician or your orthopedic doctor. You may even go straight to the Emergency Department, where X-rays will be obtained.

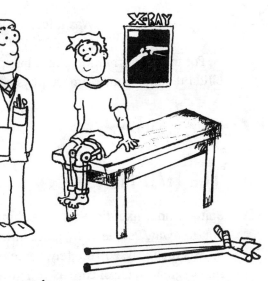

Contractures

Contractures form when muscles tighten up, making it impossible to move in a certain way. Contractures can form from muscle imbalances and/or lack of use. They are particularly common, therefore, in people who spend a lot of time in the wheelchair.

Contractures can sometimes be prevented or loosened through exercise and bracing. Sometimes an orthopedic surgeon will do surgery to loosen the tight muscle.

Degenerative Joint Disease

A joint is a space where two or more bones come together. Joints help us to move our body certain ways. For example, joints make it possible for us to bend at the elbow or knee. All joints degenerate with use and age and can become sore and stiff. Sometimes the way people with spina bifida walk puts extra pressure on their joints, making them more prone to joint problems sooner. Walking and doing things can become painful and tiresome.

Rest and medicine are used to treat joint problems. Sometimes surgery is necessary to repair or replace a joint with artificial devices that work in ways similar to a joint.

ALLERGY TO LATEX

Recently, it has been discovered that many people with spina bifida are allergic to latex (natural rubber). Allergic reactions can range from watery, itchy eyes, a skin rash, coughing, and sneezing, to a possible severe reaction, which can lead to death. Many products in the hospital (rubber gloves) and in the community (balloons) contain latex. It is important to avoid latex products as much as possible by using substitute products (vinyl, plastic, silicone). The Spina Bifida Association publishes a list of common latex products. For a copy, send a self-addressed envelope to:

> Spina Bifida Association of America
> 4590 MacArthur Blvd., N.W., Suite 250
> Washington, DC 20007-4226
> (800-621-3141)

For more information about latex and what it means to you, talk to your spina bifida team or your primary physician.

Conclusion

The Bad News

Spina bifida, like diabetes or asthma, is a chronic disability. This means it will not go away. People with spina bifida need to see their family doctors and specialists regularly. Fortunately, some problems can be lessened or prevented if you seek regular medical care as you grow older. Find a doctor you like and trust and see him as often as necessary. Take care of yourself!

The Good News

You can live a long and fulfilling life with spina bifida. Many people with spina bifida go on to college and successful careers. People with spina bifida fall in love and marry just like anyone else. Some go on to have children. Recently, federal laws such as the Americans with Disabilities Act have helped make it easier to obtain jobs and live in the community. Thanks to medical advances and changes in the way society treats individuals with disabilities, you can hope for a future with endless possibilities.

Taking Care of Business

(Self Care)

Linda Custis-Allen, M.S., OTR/L

Are you ready for a job, college, life on your own? The first step toward these goals is learning to take care of yourself.

Why is it so hard? Have you ever seen an athlete in a wheelchair competing in a marathon? Have you ever seen a dancer, a journalist, or a doctor in a wheelchair? Did you ever see a picture of President Franklin D. Roosevelt? (He used a wheelchair, you know.) Did you ever think about whether learning self-care was hard for these people, too? Well, it probably was.

People with physical disabilities often have difficulty learning to take care of themselves. You may have trouble:

◎ If your parents still do things for you because it is faster and easier. (They may not think about your need to learn and practice these skills.)

◎ Because your parents may not know how to teach you self care. They may not know about special equipment or special ways of doing things (techniques).

◎ Because learning to take care of yourself is more difficult if you have physical limitations. Yes, learning to take care of yourself is hard, but *you* can do it.

How Do You Learn Self-Care?

You can follow these four steps for learning to take care of yourself:

- ◎ **Believe**
- ◎ **Explore**
- ◎ **Plan**
- ◎ **Practice**

BELIEVE

Believe that you can learn self-care. Develop an independent attitude.

EXPLORE

Find out about special equipment and special ways of doing self-care.

1. If you have an occupational therapist, physical therapist, or nurse at school or clinic, ask them for help. Tell them what problems you are having with self-care. Ask them to help you learn to take care of yourself.

2. If you have friends with spina bifida, ask how they are doing. They may have great ideas about learning self-care.

3. Call the store or pharmacy where you get your catheters or other health supplies. Ask them if they have a catalog of self-care equipment that you can look at.

4. Visit a home health care or medical equipment store. To find a store near you, look in the yellow pages of your phone book under Hospital Equipment. Ask the salesperson to talk to you about what is available to help you with your particular problem. Sometimes the store will let you borrow equipment to try at home. Do not *buy* anything unless you *know* it will work for you!

PLAN

Make a plan for taking care of yourself. Think about:

- ◎ How you move, reach, bend, balance.
- ◎ How you learn new ways of doing things.
- ◎ How your house is arranged. (Can you get your wheelchair into the bathroom? Where is your bedroom? Do you have to go up and down steps?)

◎ The kinds of equipment available.

◎ What resources (money) you have for buying equipment or making changes to your home, such as a wider doorway, adding a ramp, etc.

For example, a tub bench may seem like the answer to your bathing problems. But it will only be the answer if...

◎ Your balance is good enough to sit without falling;

◎ You can learn how to use it safely;

◎ It will fit in your bathroom;

◎ It is the right design for you;

◎ You have the money to pay for it, or insurance to cover the cost.

That is why thinking ahead and making a PLAN is so important.

You can get help with your plan at school. Attend your individualized education program (IEP) meetings. If you are in junior high or high school, these meetings can help outline a plan for becoming independent with self-care skills. This is a chance for you, your family, and school staff to meet, identify needs, and set goals. To help you take care of yourself at school, the school is responsible for:

◎ providing a place for your self-care needs

◎ releasing you from class

◎ providing supervision or assistance as needed

◎ reinforcing procedures learned at home, clinic, or in therapy.

PRACTICE

After you get a new piece of special equipment or learn a new way of doing self-care, you'll need to practice to become independent. It may seem to take too long or be too hard at first, but practice and it will get easier.

Learning Dressing

Most people with spina bifida can dress themselves. If dressing is hard for you, here are some tips:

DRESSING IDEAS

1. Pull-on clothes like sweat suits and dresses are easier because they stretch and do not have fasteners.

2. Velcro or slip-on shoes are generally easier than shoes that tie. If you wear braces, make sure the shoes you buy can be worn with your braces.

3. Bigger sizes go on and off easier than smaller sizes.

4. Before you buy a piece of clothing, think about how you will get it on and off.

5. You may want to consider buying clothing that can be machine washed easily. Look at the care label for cleaning instructions.

6. Dressing is easier for people who are strong and flexible. Read Chapter 13 for ideas about increasing your strength and flexibility.

7. If you need a special size or special design, find someone who can sew. Tell that person what you need. Ask how much it will cost. Having your clothes made for you might be the answer. Learning to sew and make your own clothes can be an answer, too.

8. Some companies specialize in clothing and accessories for people with different needs. Here is a short list.

> **Adaptogs** offers a variety of men's and women's clothing and will work with you to develop custom features. Call for a catalog.
>
> > Adaptogs, Inc.
> > 201 North Washington
> > P.O. Box 339,
> > Otis, CO 80743
> > 1-800-535-8247
>
> **Aviano U.S.A.** offers clothing for people who sit in wheelchairs. They will also make some designs out of your fabric. Call for a catalog.
>
> > Aviano U.S.A.
> > 1199-K Avenida Acaso
> > Camarillo, CA 93012
> > 1-800-848-2837
>
> **Hen's Nest** offers custom-made clothing. Call for a brochure to find out about designs and prices.
>
> > Hen's Nest
> > P.O. Box 531
> > Colby, KS 67701
> > 1-913-462-3104
>
> **Laurel Designs** offers special clothing for adults. Call for a catalog.
>
> > Laurel Designs
> > 5 Laurel Ave.
> > Belvedere, CA 94920
> > 1-415-435-1891

Special Clothes offers a limited adult line of clothing, and children's clothes up to size 20. Call for a catalog.

> Special Clothes
> P.O. Box 333
> East Harwich, MA 02645
> 1-508-430-5172

Wheelies Bentwear offers clothing for men and women with a patented "bent" design. Call for information.

> Wheelies Bentwear
> P.O. Box 2296
> Winston, OR 97496
> 1-503-679-2318

People with spina bifida can wear stylish, appropriate, practical clothes.

DRESSING TECHNIQUES (SPECIAL WAYS)

1. Some people with spina bifida find that sitting in bed or on the floor with their legs straight in front of them allows them to reach their feet to put on pants, socks, braces, or shoes.

2. Other people find that they can place one leg bent over the other to reach one foot and then the other.

3. Sitting in a corner or against the head of the bed can help with balance while reaching.

4. Many find that to pull their pants up they must then lie down and roll side to side.

5. If one of your arms or legs is stronger or easier to move, use the following rules:

   ◎ Dress the hard side first, then the easy side.
   ◎ Undress the easy side first, then the hard side.

DRESSING EQUIPMENT

Most people with spina bifida do not need special equipment for dressing. If you do have trouble with dressing, however, equipment might help.

1. A **long handle shoe horn** can help you reach to get your foot in your shoe.

2. **Reaching devices** can help you reach your feet for dressing.

3. **Sock donners** can help you get your socks started on your feet.

4. **Dressing sticks** and aids can help you with pulling on or pushing off your clothing in hard to reach places.

(See **Explore** on page 12 of this chapter for suggestions for finding out about this equipment.)

Learning Transfers

If you use a wheelchair for getting around, it's important to be able to move in and out of your chair. This is called a *transfer*. You can transfer by standing and turning on your legs, or by using your arms to lift and move your lower body. If you can transfer to and from your bed, the toilet, bath/shower, and the floor, taking care of yourself will be much easier.

If you have trouble with any of these transfers, here are some tips:

TRANSFER IDEAS

Learning transfers begins with choosing the right wheelchair. Swing away/removable arm rests and swing away/removable foot rests will allow you to position your wheelchair very close to the surface to which you are transferring.

There is no right or wrong way to do a transfer. You must find a way that is *safe* and works for you. In a safe transfer, you keep your balance and you protect your skin from rubbing or scratches.

Transfers are easier for people who are strong and flexible.

TYPES OF TRANSFERS

Here are three different types of transfers:

Lateral Transfer to Bed

1. Position your wheelchair at a slight angle to the bed.
2. Lock the wheelchair brakes.
3. Remove the armrest closest to the bed.
4. Push down with your arms and lift your body sideways onto the bed.

Forward Transfer to Bed

1. Position your wheelchair so it is facing the bed.
2. Swing away the foot rests.
3. Lift one leg and then the other onto bed.
4. Wheel your wheelchair forward so it is as close as possible to the bed.
5. Lock the wheelchair brakes.
6. Push down with your arms and lift your body forward onto the bed.

Pivot Transfer to Bed

1. Position your wheelchair at a slight angle to the bed.
2. Lock the wheelchair brakes.
3. Swing away the foot rests.
4. Push down with your arms to move your body to the front edge of your wheelchair seat.
5. Stand up on your legs with one hand on your wheelchair and one hand on the bed.
6. Turn your body to sit on the bed.

TRANSFER EQUIPMENT

Many people with spina bifida do not need special equipment for transfers. However, depending on what you are having trouble with, some equipment might help.

Transfer boards provide a surface on which to move from one place to another. Place one end of the transfer board under your bottom and one end on the surface to which you are moving. Use your arms to lift and move your lower body across the board.

Grab bars are attached to the wall, bed, or bathtub to help you with balance and to provide you with something to hold onto so you can lift your bottom and legs.

Steps can be made for helping you get from your wheelchair to the floor and from the floor back into your wheelchair. Your wheelchair footrest can help you move down to the floor and back.

Lifts for getting in and out of a car or van, bathtub, swimming pool, etc., are available. Different kinds of lifts might be helpful, depending upon what you need to transfer to or from. Your therapist or nurse can help you decide what type of lift you need.

Ramps are inclines for moving your wheelchair up and down a number of steps or into a van. Ready-made ramps are sold by some medical equipment stores, but may not work in all situations. For a home with several steps at the entrance, a specially built ramp might be necessary. There are important guidelines for building ramps. One recommendation is that the ramp should slope upwards gradually so that you can propel your wheelchair up the ramp independently. Ideally, the ramp should rise one inch in height for every twelve inches of length. Talk to your occupational therapist, physical therapist, or other rehabilitation professional for additional guidelines on ramp construction.

WHAT ABOUT THE BATHROOM?

Many people with spina bifida find getting to and using the tub and toilet difficult. To successfully take a bath or use the toilet, special equipment or techniques are often necessary. (See **Explore** on page 12 for suggestions for finding out about this equipment.) In addition, home or bathroom modifications (changes) might be needed.

Special Equipment

The **shower wheelchair** has brakes, swing-away foot rests, and arm rests. You can propel it just like a regular wheelchair. It also has a cut-out seat for use over a standard toilet, and is made of water-resistant material for use in a roll-in shower.

The **commode chair** is a chair with a cut-out seat and a pail or bucket underneath. It can be used in the bathroom or the bedroom and comes in a variety of styles: drop arm rests, wheeled or stationary, adjustable leg height, etc.

The **raised toilet seat** is a device that attaches to a standard toilet to make the seat the same height as your wheelchair. This makes transfers easier.

A **hydraulic bath lift** looks like a cot inside your tub. It provides a surface for transfer and uses water pressure to lower the person down into the tub and raise the person back out of the tub after bathing.

The **transfer bench** is a bench that is positioned across the bath tub so that there is no gap between the tub and the bench. You transfer onto the bench and wash yourself with a hand-held or overhead shower. It comes in a variety of styles: with or without back rests, padded seat, arm rests, etc.

The **shower seat** is a chair or bench that is used inside the tub.

Grab bars can be mounted or positioned to help with balance and body movement.

A **long-handled sponge** may be used to help reach your back or feet for washing.

Nonskid bath mats and strips help prevent sliding and loss of balance for those who are able to get down into and out of the bathtub. Be sure these products are not made of latex. (For information about latex allergy, read Chapter 1.).

◎ ◎ ◎ ◎ ◎

"The hardest thing about taking care of myself is bathing, because it is hard to reach different parts of my body." —E.B.

Home Modifications

Home modifications are often necessary so that you can use your wheelchair in the bathroom. This might be as simple as making a door wider, or as complicated as adding a first-floor bathroom.

Some local agencies might help finance these modifications. You may also be able to deduct the cost from your income tax. Check with a tax accountant or call the Internal Revenue Service about this possibility. You can find the phone number for the

Internal Revenue Service in the white pages under United States Government Internal Revenue Service. Ask the representative about your specific question and request a copy of Internal Revenue Service Publication 502. Publication 502 provides information about deducting expenses for required home improvements.

If you are thinking about home modifications, obtain the assistance of an occupational therapist, physical therapist, or rehab nurse to help you consider all possibilities.

Make sure you work with a carpenter, contractor, or architect who knows about modifications for people with disabilities.

If home modifications are too expensive or if you (or your family) are thinking about moving, consider moving to housing which is already equipped and accessible for people with disabilities.

Don't Give Up

If you have read this chapter, tried the suggestions, and still have difficulty with self-care, **Don't Give Up!** There are other opportunities for you.

Think about a hospital admission for physical rehabilitation. Talk to your primary care physician about this. A hospital admission for physical rehabilitation could help you:

- ◎ maximize your physical ability for self-care (strength, balance, mobility);
- ◎ learn and practice new ways of doing things;
- ◎ try out and order special equipment;
- ◎ decide on home modifications or find an accessible place to live;
- ◎ find assisted living or attendant care if you need it.

Or, you might decide to hire an attendant to help you with whatever activity you just can't perform by yourself. To find attendant care, look in the yellow pages of your phone book under Home Health Services, or call one of the agencies listed in Chapter 11. These agencies can help you identify financial resources to pay for an attendant.

If you do decide to try attendant care, don't feel as if you're somehow settling for less independence. Remember, "Independence is a State of Mind." Knowing what you need and getting it *is* independence. Develop an independent attitude! Take care of business!

(3)

Caring for Your Largest Organ

(Skin Care)

Marlene Lutkenhoff, R.N., M.S.N.

What Shape Is Your Skin In?

It is important to keep your skin in tiptop condition. Skin protects the muscle tissue and blood vessels below it. Skin that is open or has holes in it permits germs to get inside the body where they don't belong.

Pressure Sores

Pressure sores are injuries to the skin. Sometimes they start out as a change in the color of your skin, but they can develop into big openings. They usually occur in areas that take a lot of pressure or force from your body, such as the hips, butt, ankles, feet, and heels.

People with spina bifida are more likely to develop pressure sores for several reasons. First, if they cannot feel pressure, pain, or wetness on parts of their body, they may not know when to move or when to change underclothes. Second, if they have trouble moving around, they may sit for long periods of time.

This puts a lot of pressure on the skin, and blood vessels beneath the skin get squeezed. Oxygen has a hard time getting to skin cells when vessels are squeezed. Without oxygen, skin cells will die. People with spina bifida may also have trouble with pressure sores due to bowel and bladder accidents. If accidents are frequent and the individual does not get cleaned up quickly, the skin becomes irritated and may break open.

Finally, if the person with spina bifida is heavy or overweight, sitting or standing puts extra pressure on areas that may break down, such as the butt or feet. Extra weight means extra pressure.

13 Ways to Help Keep Your Skin at Its Best

1. **Keep your body CLEAN.** Wash daily with soaps that are as close to the pH of the skin as possible, such as Neutrogena, Basis, and Alveeno. Dry yourself well before putting on your clothes.

2. **MOVE your body.** If you are in a wheelchair, lift your butt off the seat of your wheelchair every 15 minutes. If you are watching television, that means lift during each commercial. If you are in class at school, that means lift at least four times during that class. A watch that beeps every 15 minutes might help remind you to lift. If you cannot lift your whole butt off the seat, then lift one side at a time.

3. **LOOK at your body.** Inspect your skin *daily*. Pay special attention to the parts of your body you do not feel. Use a mirror to help you see and be sure you are in a room with good lighting. Look for discoloration, swelling, open areas, and drainage. Also, be aware of moles on your body. At least once a month, check them for color or size changes.

4. **Apply CREAMS or LUBRICANTS** to your skin after bathing so your skin doesn't become dry and cracked.

5. **Do not slide to transfer.** It is best to LIFT your body when moving from one place to another.

6. **Remove wet or dirty underclothes as soon as possible.** WASH and DRY yourself carefully after bowel or bladder accidents.

7. **Be sure pants, skirts, shoes, and socks all FIT properly.** Be careful of zippers on pants and skirts.

8. **Be sure your body FITS in your wheelchair or in your braces properly.**

9. **Use a PRESSURE RELIEF CUSHION** in your wheelchair or on any hard seat you will be sitting on. These cushions can be ordered from the place you got your wheelchair from. They are like a pillow for your rear end.

10. **Burns are often avoidable.**

 ◎ Use precaution when handling hot liquids or hot utensils by wearing oven mitts.

 ◎ Take care when bathing. Test the temperature of the water with your hands before getting into the bathtub. Do not add hot water while you are sitting in the tub. Otherwise, you might burn parts of your legs and butt where you have decreased feelings.

 ◎ Apply sun screen lotion with a sun protection factor of 8 to 15 to all exposed skin before spending time in the sun. You may not feel your legs getting burned, so adequate protection is essential.

 ◎ Metals get hot in warm weather. Be careful of the metal on seatbelt buckles, metal footrests on wheelchairs, and any metal surfaces. If you have any decreased sensation in your feet, do not go barefoot.

 ◎ A burn results in red skin. If it is bad enough, it will blister. Eventually, the blisters will open and infections are possible. If the skin is just red, apply cool, wet dressings to the affected area. If the skin blisters or appears to worsen, see a physician for treatment.

 ◎ People taking drugs that relax the bladder (Ditropan™, Tofranil™, Probanthine™, or Benadryl™) need to be aware that these drugs can cause decreased sweating. As a result, you may become overheated quickly. Try wearing a hat in the summer sun and avoid being out in the sun from 11:00 A.M. to 3:00 P.M., if possible.

11. **Eat wisely and NUTRITIOUSLY.** Foods like cantaloupe, carrots, spinach, greens, oranges, tomatoes, strawberries, fish, cereals, lean meat, and milk will help provide the vitamins and minerals you need for healthy skin.

12. **DRINK** eight glasses of water a day to help keep your skin moist.

13. **Consider MOISTURE BARRIERS on skin frequently exposed to urine.** These can be obtained at a medical supply store.

Why Bother?

It is easier to prevent pressure sores than to treat them. Treatment is costly. Treatment may include bed rest, hospitalization, or plastic surgery. A severe pressure sore may result in the loss of a body part or even death. Pressure sores can take a long time to heal. Instead of being out with friends, at school, or at work, you may be lying flat on your stomach at home or in the hospital.

TREATMENT

If you notice a reddened or discolored area, keep tight clothing and braces off and stay off the affected area until normal color returns. Try to figure out what caused the redness or color change and take care of the situation. If skin is broken or redness fails to disappear, see a physician. A doctor may prescribe any of the following methods. Treatment depends on the degree of damage to the tissue.

"Getting a pressure sore is inconvenient. It limits your ability to do what you want to do. If you do get one, the best advice is to stay off it as much as possible." - Adam

Pressure Relief

The doctor may require you to be off the sore completely. Depending on where the pressure sore is, this could mean lying on your stomach or side instead of sitting or lying on your back. Why? To allow greater flow of oxygen and nutrients to the area.

Skin Protection

Sometimes ointments, sprays, or dressings are recommended for open wounds. This protects the skin from moisture or wetness and promotes healing. Ask your physician about using either a hydrogel, hydrocolloid, or transparent film dressing.

Frequent Cleansing

Mild soap or water or a particular wound cleanser may be recommended for draining wounds. This can help promote wound healing. Ask your physician about using a hypertonic dressing or calcium alginate. Caution: Never use Betadine or Hydrogen Perioxide on a pressure sore.

Debridement

This refers to removal of dead skin tissues. Ways to do this include:
◎ Surgical—cutting and removing dead tissue.

◎ Chemical—use of medications that digest and loosen dead tissue.

Debridement will probably not hurt you because you have decreased sensation in this area. That is why you got the pressure sore to begin with.

Special Diets and Vitamin Supplements

People with pressure sores lose significant amounts of protein through the wound. For this reason, a high protein diet may be recommended. You may also be given Vitamin C and zinc supplements, as they help wounds to heal.

Are You at Risk for Skin Problems?

Directions: Read the statements and answer true or false.

	True	False
1. I look at my body every day to check for sores or irritations.		
2. I am careful to remove wet or dirty underclothes after accidents.		
3. I always check my bath water with my hands before getting in the tub.		
4. I eat nutritiously, choosing foods from all food groups. (Milk group, fruit and vegetable group, bread and cereal group, meat-egg-bean-nut group)		
5. I move around a lot either by walking or by lifting my butt off the seat of my wheelchair about every 15 minutes.		
6. I drink 6 to 8 glasses of water a day.		
TOTAL		

If you answered true to these statements, you are doing a great job in caring for your skin. If you answered false to one or more statements, make a decision to change and begin TODAY!

Solid Waste

(The Bowels)

Roberta Hills, R.N., M.S.

Most people don't need to give a second thought to how their bowels work. They put food in their body at one end (their mouth), and then presto! The portion of the food not needed by their body exits through the other end with a minimum of fuss. Unfortunately, this process is not usually so easy and troublefree for people with spina bifida. People with spina bifida usually have difficulties with muscle control and sensation in the bowel area. As a result, they need to consciously learn to manage their bowels.

How Do the Bowels Work for Most People?

To understand why it is harder for you to manage your bowels, it helps to understand how they work ordinarily. After you eat something, the food gets chewed and digested, making a watery mush. Water and nutrients from the mush are absorbed in the intestine. The remaining body waste is called stool.

Stool makes its way out of the body through the bowels. There are three main muscles related to the bowels: the colon, rectum, and anus. The *colon* or large intestine is a tube for passage of bowel movements or stool. The *rectum* is a storage area. The *anus* allows for passage of stool out of the body. Nerves to the muscles cause movement and feeling.

Want to see how muscles and nerves work together? Make yourself swallow. (You will have to send a message from your brain to your nerves to do this.) You can feel muscles in the back of your mouth move and touch the top of your throat.

How Does the Food Get through the Tube?

Peristalsis is muscle activity that pushes food through the tube (colon). It is a squeezing and relaxing of the intestinal tube, like squeezing toothpaste out of a tube.

The stool is squeezed into the rectum from the colon. Once inside the rectum, the stool stretches nerve fibers there. This causes a sensation that lets people know they need to have a bowel movement.

The stool leaves the body through the anus. The walls of the anal tube lie snugly together, keeping the stool from coming out. When you grunt, bear down, laugh, cough, or sneeze, stool is pushed out.

The anus has sensory nerves that let most people know when stool is there. If they are not near a toilet, most people can tighten up the sphincter muscle in the anus and keep the stool from passing out of the body. People with spina bifida usually cannot tighten this sphincter.

The sphincter muscle is like your lip muscles. To understand how it works, tighten and pucker your lips. Now, relax and open your lips.

Common Questions about the Bowels

Q. What is the most likely time for a bowel movement to occur?
A. Bowel movements tend to occur with activity, such as going from asleep to awake. Having something warm to eat or drink also helps.

Q. How long does it take for the food you eat to leave the body?
A. Food you eat is out of the body in five days.

Q. Why do diarrhea and constipation occur?
A. Normal stool is firm and sausage-like. *Diarrhea,* or watery stool, results when digested food passes through the body too quickly. *Constipation* occurs when the stool sits in the colon too long. Water is absorbed from the stool, resulting in hard balls.

Q. What is the average number of bowel movements for most persons?
A. The average is from three a day to three a week. It depends on what you eat and how active you are. Fewer than three bowel movements a week is considered a sign of constipation.

What Happens to People Born with Spina Bifida?

People who are born with spina bifida have a stretched and damaged spinal cord. The scar on your back shows the level of the damage. Nerves below the scar are also damaged.

Most people with spina bifida have problems feeling the stool in the anus because the nerves that go to the bowel are not functioning. Most cannot tighten the sphincter muscle which keeps the stool from coming out.

NOT ALL PEOPLE BORN WITH SPINA BIFIDA ARE ALIKE!

Some people have what is called a tight anus. This means the muscles in the anus stay snugly together until the rectum is full of stool. These people have few accidents if they do their bowel program every day or every other day.

Other people have what is called a loose anus. Once stool enters the rectum, it slips into the anus and out of the body. These kids have to do their bowel program daily. They also have to check their bowels before activities such as lifting, walking, running, or playing ball. They go to the bathroom, push, grunt, and may need to use a gloved finger to remove any stool in reach.

Some people with spina bifida have a sensation that lets them know that they have to go to the bathroom. This may be a feeling of fullness, gurgling, slight wetting, or leg twitching. To prevent an accident, these people have to get to the bathroom right away.

Everyone needs to learn to respond to their body's messages. For instance, passing gas is a message that there is movement going on in the colon. How should you respond? Go to the toilet and see if you can pass stool.

Eight Things You Must Learn

1. **Learn about your body.** Use a mirror to look at your bottom. Where do you have feeling? Touch lightly, then touch firmly. If you can't feel your fingers when you touch or pinch, then these areas need extra care. Look at the skin every day for spots or sores.

2. Learn how your body reacts to foods and medications. For example, some people find that chocolate causes loose stools. Some people have bowel movements after eating a large meal, so may want to eat smaller meals. Ditropan™, which is used to help relax the bladder so it can hold more urine, causes constipation. Drinking extra water can help. So can eating foods such as wheat bran, fruits, and vegetables with skins.

3. Learn how your body reacts to activity. If you have a bowel movement in gym or with physical activity, use the toilet before the activity starts.

4. Check to see if there is a pattern to your bowel movements. Do you have bowel movements in the morning? afternoon? evening? or in the bathtub?

If there is a pattern, plan your bowel program around your body pattern. If you do not know your pattern, spend two weeks recording the time of day you have bowel movements so you can see if you have a pattern. If you do not seem to have a pattern, a good time to do your bowel program might be one-half hour after your evening meal.

5. Learn to check your underwear and pads for a bowel movement. If it smells like stool, excuse yourself, go to the bathroom and check. Be the first to know!

TIPS ON CHECKING YOURSELF

1. Learn the smell of your bowel movement.
2. Feel your bottom, using a tissue.
3. If you see stool on the tissue, get to the toilet. Try to grunt and push stool out. Change soiled clothes and place in a plastic bag.
4. If cleaning up is too difficult, figure out how to get help or how to get home quick.

TIPS ON CLEAN-UP

1. Carry adequate supplies (washcloth, towel, absorbent pads, plastic bag, mirror, and change of undergarments).
2. Check bathrooms for accessibility.
3. Wet your washcloth. Remove soiled clothes. Wash behind and between your legs as you roll from side to side.
4. Use a mirror to check your progress.

6. **Learn how to get cleaned up when accidents occur.** Practice at home to find out what works for you.

7. **Learn to ask for what you need.** Before the first week of school, find out which bathroom is available for you. Make sure it offers privacy and plenty of space. Check out the bathroom. Find out who is available to assist you if need be.

8. **Learn what kind of bowel program works best for you.** (See the information below about different kinds of bowel programs.) If you have more than two bowel accidents a month, your bowel program is not working well for you.

What Is the Goal of a Bowel Program?

The goal of a bowel program is to empty the colon of stool before it surprises you and empties on its own, causing a bowel accident.

FOUR PRINCIPLES FOR EFFECTIVE BOWEL PROGRAMS

1. Patience and Humor. A bowel program takes time and hard work. Once you think it is working, an accident occurs. A good sense of humor is helpful. Stick with a bowel program at least three months to see if you can regulate your body.

2. Routine. Routine refers to doing your bowel program daily at about the same time. Meals and medications should also be eaten or taken at about the same time each day.

Some kids are able to do their program every other day. Once a week is not enough. Why? Build-up of stool can cause:

◎ Damage to nerves in the rectum
◎ Diarrhea
◎ Bladder infections

3. Firm Formed Stool. Stool should be like sausage links. Bowel programs do not work well when the stool is loose or like hard balls. To firm up loose stool, eat soluble fiber (beans, oatmeal, broccoli, barley, or oat bran). Soluble fiber thickens in water, slowing down the passage of stool. To soften hard stool, eat insoluble fiber, such as fruit and vegetables with their skins on and wheat bran. Insoluble fiber is the woody parts of plants, which speeds the passage of stool through the body. Drink plenty of water.

4. Exercise/Activity. Body movement moves stool through the body and improves muscle tone. Examples of good exercises are belly massage and push ups.

What Are the Different Bowel Programs?

Bowel programs differ in the amount of control they give you over when you have a bowel movment. The programs that give you the most control involve applying direct action on the anus and rectum. Bowel programs include:

1. Sitting on the pot for 20-30 minutes, pushing and grunting.

2. Laxatives. They are taken by mouth, so there is less control as to when they will work.

3. Digital stimulation. This is done by moving a gloved finger in a circular motion to stretch the anus. For best results, push and bear down at the same time.

4. Suppository. This is made of a waxy substance that contains chemicals. It looks like a bullet and is the size of your little finger. The suppository melts when placed in the anus. Suppositories help you have a bowel movement.

5. Enema. This is a liquid that is put in the anus. It can act as a wash out or react with muscles to cause a bowel movement.

Many people with spina bifida combine techniques. For instance, some people may take a laxative in the morning. In the evening, they sit on the toilet and grunt. Then they may use a gloved finger to stimulate a bowel movement.

Or, some people may put a suppository in before dinner, then lie flat to let it melt. After dinner, they sit on the toilet to grunt, push, or use digital stimulation to get the bowel movement started.

"The hardest thing about taking care of myself is fitting a bowel program into my daily routine. I have trouble giving myself an enema, too." - JMP

Tips on Using Suppositories

1. Remove stool in lower anus (Put on a vinyl glove, apply K-Y Jelly or Lubrifax, and pull out stool from anus.)

2. Slip the suppository against the wall of the anus, not into stool.

3. Push the suppository up as high as possible. Lie on your left side and bear down as you push up.

4. Lie flat or tape the buttocks for 30 minutes to give it time to melt.

5. Sit on the toilet and try to have a bowel movement.

Enema Tips

1. Remove stool in lower anus.

2. Put the fluid in as you lie on your left side with right leg bent, or on your knees with buttocks in the air.

3. Hold the buttocks together while you let the fluid in. Give the enema slowly. You will have trouble holding the fluid in, especially if it is a high volume enema (lots of fluid), so give yourself the enema some place where leakage won't matter. Once the fluid is in, sit on the toilet and grunt.

How Are You Doing with Your Bowel Movement?

	Yes	No
1. Do you have bowel accidents less than two times a month?		
2. Can you clean yourself up after a bowel accident?		
3. Do you have a bowel program that you do on a routine basis?		
4. Are you doing your own bowel program?		
5. Do you know what foods or medicines cause you to have diarrhea?		
6. Do you know what foods or medicines cause you to be constipated?		
7. Do you know what foods to eat to get your stools to be soft and firm, like sausage links?		
TOTAL		

If you answered "yes" to all of these questions, you are in great shape! If you answered "no" to any of these questions, you have some work to do. **START TODAY** to learn about your body and practice managing your bowel program.

(5)

Water-works

(Care of Your Urinary Tract)

Nan Tobias, M.S.N., R.N., CS, P.N.P.

Most people with spina bifida have difficulty with bladder control. They usually have problems with *incontinence* (urine leakage) and are prone to urinary tract infections. You may wonder how to go about becoming more independent in your toileting needs or how to avoid urinary tract infections. That's what this chapter is all about.

What the Urinary System Looks Like

The urinary tract includes the kidneys, ureters, bladder, and urethra. Kidneys are brownish red, bean-shaped organs that filter your blood and clean out waste. They work very much like the filter in a swimming pool. Things that you wouldn't want in your swimming pool, like dirt, twigs, and leaves, are cleaned out by pumping the water through the swimming pool filter. Similarly, things that your body doesn't need, like excess water, salts, and other waste products, are cleaned out by the kidneys as blood is pumped through them.

The kidneys are connected to the urinary bladder by two hollow tubes called ureters. The urine (pee) is made by the kidneys, travels down the ureters, and empties into the bladder. The bladder is a round organ made out of muscle. As the bladder fills with urine, its walls stretch. This happens much like a balloon stretches as it is filled with water. Once the bladder reaches a certain level of fullness, it sends a message to the brain that says, "I'm full! Please empty me."

The brain responds by telling the person to get to the bathroom. If the person is wise, that is where he will soon be. The urine then leaves the bladder through a tube called the urethra.

How Does Spina Bifida Affect the Urinary Tract?

In order for the brain to get word that the bladder is full, a message has to be sent. That is done by the spinal cord. The spinal cord is a long, thin tube that is located in the middle of your back. Nerves, or message lines, run up and down inside it. This system works a lot like your telephone. A message comes into your house along telephone wires and your phone rings.

When the urinary bladder is full, it sends a message to the brain along the spinal cord. The brain receives the message and tells the body to get to the bathroom.

What do you think might happen if some of the telephone wires didn't work well? If a few of the wires became disconnected, your telephone would not ring. Similarly, if the nerves in the spinal cord are not connected as they are meant to be, the bladder cannot tell when it is full. This is what happens in people with spina bifida.

Because the bladder cannot sense when it is full, it can't tell the brain (by way of the spinal cord) to get to the bathroom. The bladder's muscle wall doesn't stretch very well either and can become stiff and rigid. It is much like trying to blow up a balloon that won't let the air in.

Normally, urine flows in one direction—out of the body. In people with spina bifida, though, urine can also flow back up into the kidneys. This is because the spinal nerves don't send or receive messages well, so the wall of the bladder can become extremely stiff. When this happens, the bladder forces urine that has drained down into it from the kidneys to go back up again. This is called *vesicoureteral reflux* (or reflux for short). If not treated, reflux can lead to kidney infections and kidney damage.

The bladder muscle can get spasms which can be quite strong and can cause urine to leak out the urethra. Urine can also leak out because the nerve control at the opening and closing of the urethra is interrupted.

Urinary Tract Infections

Infections caused by bacteria (germs) can occur inside the bladder or in the kidneys, or both. If you have a bladder infection, you may not feel very sick. If you have a kidney infection, though, you may become so ill that you need to have IV fluids and IV antibiotics. If you become this sick, you will probably need to be in a hospital for a few days.

In order to keep your urinary tract healthy and help prevent infections, follow these guidelines:

1. Keep your skin clean and free from urine and bowel movements. There are germs in bowel movements, and germs grow in urine if it is left on your skin or clothes for long periods. The germs can travel into your bladder and cause a bladder infection. If you have reflux, the germs can travel to your kidneys and cause a kidney infection. Even if you don't have reflux, you can sometimes get a kidney infection.

2. Drink at least two liters of water and juice daily. Doing this will help flush out any germs that may get into your bladder.

3. Stay away from foods and liquids that can harm your bladder and cause it to work less well. These things include soft drinks or anything else with carbonation—the bubbles in soda or some bottled water. They also include tea, coffee, or anything else with caffeine, as well as chocolate and citrus. Citrus includes grapefruit, oranges, lemons, limes, and tomatoes. This also includes their juices. This does not mean you can never again have these foods and fluids. It means that it is better for your body to have healthier fluids and that the above-mentioned items should be considered treats and only consumed on special occasions.

4. Follow your bowel program. If your bowels are being emptied regularly, your bladder will work better. Your bowels and bladder are located very close together in your abdomen. If your bowels become too full and don't work well, they will push on your bladder and make it leak more and work less well.

Checking Up On Your Urinary Tract

Everyone with spina bifida should have a *urologist*. A urologist is a doctor who helps keep your urinary tract healthy. Every once in a while, the urologist will need to have special tests done of your urinary tract.

WHAT TESTS WILL YOU HAVE?

Renal Ultrasound

One test you will have is called ultrasound. This test involves taking pictures of kidneys, ureters, and bladders with sound waves. It is a very simple exam and is painless. A technician will place a warm, soothing liquid on your back and abdomen and rub them with a wand that looks something like a microphone. An image will be shown on a screen and special pictures will be developed. The pictures will show whether there is any swelling or scarring in your kidneys or ureters, whether the wall of the bladder looks normal, and whether your bladder is emptied all the way after you urinate or catheterize. How often you will have this test depends on your age and what past ultrasound pictures have shown about your urinary system.

Voiding Cystourethrogram (VCUG)

Another test you will have is called a voiding cystourethrogram. This is an X-ray of your urinary tract that is taken after putting special liquid into your bladder through a catheter. The X-rays give a very close-up picture of the bladder and show whether vesicoureteral reflux (backup of urine) is present.

If you have reflux, you will need to have this test done every year or so. If you do not have reflux, it will need to be done less often.

Renal Scan

Another test you may have done is called a renal scan. This is a test that shows how well and how fast your kidneys filter your blood. It will show how much of the overall kidney work is done by each kidney. It may also show any scarring or damage that has been done to your kidneys in the past (by infection, for example).

Urodynamics

Urodynamics is a test to measure how stiff the bladder wall is. It involves passing a catheter through the urethra into the bladder. The catheter has a pressure tester on it. As water fills your bladder through the urethra, pressure readings are measured. If this test shows a very stiff bladder wall with high pressure readings, it may mean you will need daily medication to relax the bladder wall. This medicine will help keep the kidneys healthy, protect them from further damage, and keep you dry.

Not only does this test measure the stiffness of the bladder wall, but it measures how strong the urethra is. If the urethra is too weak, it will not be able to keep urine from leaking out. Certain medicines and sometimes surgery can make a weak urethra stronger.

How to Stay Dry

If your bladder leaks urine, you may need to take medicine to help stay dry. A medicine called Ditropan™ is a common medicine that many people with spina bifida take. It helps the stiff bladder wall relax. As a result, the bladder can hold more urine before it leaks. Your doctor might also prescribe other medicines that work a lot like Ditropan. These include Levsin™ and Probanthine™.

Another common problem for people with spina bifida is that the bladder does not empty totally on its own. This means they need to learn to catheterize their bladders. To do so, they insert a catheter (a hollow tube made of soft plastic) into the bladder at regular intervals during the day. This empties the bladder out. Your doctors and nurses can help you learn this procedure or help answer your questions if it is something you have done for a period of time already.

Sometimes an operation is needed to help a person stay dry. For example, surgeries can enlarge the size of the bladder and/or help strengthen the lower part of the bladder. Someone who has trouble catheterizing because of physical limitations might have a procedure called a Mitrofanoff done. This operation creates an opening on the abdomen that connects to the bladder. Instead of catheterizing the urethra, a catheter would be placed through this opening in order to empty the bladder. The point is, there are many ways to get away from using special undergarments and pads.

Day to Day Life

You may have many worries or fears about your everyday life because of how your urinary tract works. If you leak urine, you may wear pads or incontinence briefs. You may have fears about other people finding out. Feelings of shame or embarrassment are normal and should not keep you from taking part in activities. For example, if everyone is required to take group showers after physical education, you might ask your teacher to be excused from class a few minutes early in order to have some privacy. (This could be addressed on your IEP or 504 plan.) If your current way of urinary control is not working for you, ask your doctors and nurses for help. They may not be aware of your difficulties.

Many incontinence products are available on the market. Some are small disposable pads with adhesive backing that can be attached to underpants. There are also cloth reusable shields that fit onto a belt or into specially made underwear. In addition, there are thick cotton pads for people in wheelchairs that absorb urine and wash well between uses. If you are not familiar with such products, you can visit a local medical supply company and look at them.

Many companies will be happy to show you their products and discuss the benefits of each. It can be embarrassing in the beginning, but your needs in this area are lifelong and need to be addressed. It will be to your advantage to find the products that work best for *you.* If you cannot visit a medical supply store, there are mail order companies that will send out catalogues and samples of items to try.

School and Friends

One of the things that worries most people who catheterize is whether to tell friends, classmates, and teachers. You may worry that other people will find out and will make fun because you use the bathroom differently.

Whether you choose to tell others or not is an individual decision. You must feel that your choice is right for you. The choices you make, however, should not interfere with your being able to take care of your body. For example, one young man was afraid to tell his classmates and friends that he emptied his bladder differently. He would catheterize himself in the morning before he left for school and then not again until after he returned home in the afternoon. This was nine hours later! In order to keep from having a noticeable wet spot on his clothes at school, he would wear a disposable incontinence brief. This soaked up all the urine that he leaked during the day. He also did not drink very many fluids while at school and his urine would become very dark and concentrated. This was definitely not a good idea. His plan may have kept him from embarrassment, but his kidneys and bladder were in danger of infection and damage.

Can you think of better ways to handle the above situation? For example, you could tell a few close friends that you use catheters, or you might choose not to tell anyone. In that case, you might just say that you are going to the nurse's office to take medicine when you need to leave the classroom.

A Few Tips

◎ Fanny packs and backpacks make good storage places for supplies when on the go. Catheters, wet wipes or swab sticks, and a change of clothes can fit in nicely.

◎ No bathroom around? Catheterize before you leave home or in your car.

◎ Grab a paper towel or a small pad to set your supplies on when using the bathroom in the mall or another public place. You don't want to get an infection from other people's germs.

◎ If you take extra catheters, it won't matter if you accidently drop one on a dirty floor somewhere.

◎ At a friend's house and don't know what to do with your used supplies? Bring a baggie, place your supplies in the baggie, and toss it away later when convenient.

◎ When clothes are easy to get on and off, cathing is less trouble and takes less time.

◎ It's hard to remember to catheter-ize. Consider using a watch that can be set to beep at scheduled times.

◎ You will be surprised at how quickly you are able to catheterize yourself after you have practiced it for while.

◎ If you do not feel comfortable catheterizing in a public bathroom at school, your parent or nurse can talk with your teacher or principal to arrange a more private location (for example, a teacher's bathroom or health room). This issue could be addressed on your IEP or Section 504 plan.

"When I'm away from home, I make sure I bring enough catheters along. Usually, this is not a long procedure. It usually takes only one or two minutes." - JMP

What if you want to share information about yourself, but just don't know how to go about it? First of all, going to the bathroom is a fact of life. Everybody does it in one way or another.

Sometimes, though, it is very difficult to explain to other people about bathroom habits. That is because our bathroom habits are very private. On top of that, we are sometimes told or are led to believe that bathroom habits or our genitals are somehow unclean or "dirty."

Don't let other people's beliefs limit or hurt you. Being very matter of fact with others about your bathroom habits will only help you in the long run. You do not have to give more information about yourself than you are comfortable giving. For example, it is perfectly all right to tell others, "I pee by putting a tube into my bladder."

What if you just cannot bring yourself to tell others? One way you can help others understand your needs is to ask your nurse or doctor to talk to your peers. Health professionals can explain about anatomy and physiology and why your body is the way it is. You will probably even find that once others understand, they will be friendlier and even offer you their help if you need things. If people have been mean to you in the past, it is probably due to their own fears or misunderstandings.

Occasionally, some people might say or do mean things to you even when things are explained to them. If this happens, you must have a great deal of courage. One way to handle situations like this is to just ignore the mean things people say.

Another way is to confront the person and say, "Those things you said really hurt my feelings. I may walk differently than you (or look different from you) or pee differently than you, but I have the same feelings that you do. I would appreciate it if you did not say those things." Saying something like this may even get a conversation started with the person. In the end, he may learn more about you and you may learn more about him. If not, at least you will have told the person what you think. How other people respond is not in your control. That is up to them.

Summary

The care of your urinary tract is important for your overall health, as well as your social and emotional well-being. If you take care of your kidneys and bladder properly, chances are good that they will work well for as long as you need them. Likewise, if you follow healthy habits and the instructions that your nurses and doctors give you, you will be able to go places and do things with your friends with very little chance of having an accident. The time to learn good habits is now.

(6)

Walking & Wheeling

(Mobility Issues)

Catherine Lowe, M.S., P.T.

Let's Go!

Just because you have spina bifida doesn't mean you don't have choices about where and how to go . . . to a friend's house, on a date, to a football game, to your job, or on a trip around the country. Whether you go with crutches or a wheelchair, in a car or on the bus doesn't matter. More important is that you *just plain go.*

Community ambulator, household ambulator, therapeutic ambulator, and wheelchair user are words to describe people who move in different ways. Which words best describe you?

Community Ambulator: You can walk by yourself at home, school, and other places in the community. You may use braces, a walker, or crutches. You may even use a wheelchair instead of walking for long distances, like at an amusement park or at the mall, but you walk most of the time.

Household Ambulator: You walk only at home. You may walk when you're at a friend's house, too, but when you go out, you almost always use a wheelchair.

Therapeutic Ambulator: You walk only for exercise. Standing and walking, for you, may take a lot of energy, but their advantages are worth it. Standing can make your bones grow and make them strong so they don't break. It can keep your joints from getting stuck in contractures. Standing in an upright position can also improve how you breathe and how your kidneys and bladder drain. This can prevent you from getting sick.

Wheelchair User: You use a wheelchair almost all of the time at home and in the community. "Wheelchair user" doesn't mean you never get out of your chair. At home, many people transfer in and out of their wheelchairs and crawl on the floor, onto furniture, and up and down the stairs. Moving around on the floor, moving from chair to chair, and moving from the floor into your wheelchair make it possible for you to get anywhere and sit anywhere you choose, even when you're in a place that is not wheelchair accessible, like at a friend's house or while traveling.

Crutches and Walkers

If you are an "ambulator," crutches and walkers may be important tools to help you get around.

Forearm crutches are shorter and less bulky than regular crutches. Each has an armpiece that wraps around your arm between your elbow and hand. This armpiece keeps the crutch from falling off your arm when you need to hold onto a railing to go up and down the stairs. Talk to a wheelchair vendor about getting a crutch holder for your wheelchair so you can carry your crutches and get to them easily when you need them. If you feel a little unsteady on forearm crutches, consider getting bigger "jumbo" crutch tips. These look like suction cups and stick to the ground so the crutch doesn't slip.

Walkers are bigger than forearm crutches, and so are almost impossible to transport on your wheelchair. You can learn to go up and down one or two stairs with a walker, but you will have to take the elevator or use a ramp for a flight of stairs. Although walkers can limit where you move, when it comes to choosing one, the choices are limitless! A reverse walker is open in front of you instead of behind you. With a reverse walker, you can walk up to a table or work surface without the walker getting in the way. Some people sit on the back of their walker when they need a rest; others actually buy a seat from their medical supplier that turns their walker into a chair when they need one. Having a reverse walker can be like carrying a chair with you.

Most walkers have two front wheels. Little wheels tend to get stuck in grass, gravel, and carpet; bigger wheels make it easier to move the walker over the ground. If your balance makes it hard for you to pick up the walker, wheels that swivel can make turning easier. Walkers with four wheels move FAST, and some have hand brakes like bicycle brakes to help you control your speed. Finally, if you use a walker, don't forget a basket to carry your things with you!

Leg Braces

Leg braces are another kind of tool to help you get around. If you can straighten your knees by yourself, all you may need are **short leg braces**. These AFO's, or **a**nkle **f**oot **o**rthoses, can enable you to stand still by yourself without holding onto something to keep from falling. Short leg braces can also make walking look and feel less awkward. Most AFO's are lightweight plastic that mold to the back of your leg and ankle and fit inside your shoes. Although they fit under pants and skirts, some people also fold their socks down over the top of their braces to make them less obvious.

If you have trouble straightening your knees, your legs may bend so that you crouch when you walk. Short leg braces that mold to the front of your leg, or **anti-crouch AFO's**, can help you straighten your legs even if the muscles are weak.

Long leg braces are good tools for walking if the muscles that straighten your knees don't work at all. These braces are also called KAFO's, or **k**nee **a**nkle **f**oot **o**rthoses, because they extend up over your knees to keep them from bending when you stand. KAFO's are bigger than short leg braces, but they still fit under skirts and baggy pants so other people can't see them. Some people who can't move their knees *or* their hips can stand and walk using KAFO's with a tie bar. This is a piece of metal or plastic that ties their legs together. They stand leaning forward on a walker or crutches. Then, they push down with their arms and swing both legs forward. Walking this way takes a lot of balance and arm strength, but with work and practice, you can do it, too!

Even if you use a wheelchair most of the time, you may benefit from long leg braces to help with standing transfers, or AFO's to protect your feet and ankles with weight bearing transfers.

Long leg braces with a waist band are for people who need support around their hips. They are also called **HKAFO's**, or **h**ip **k**nee **a**nkle **f**oot **O**rthoses, because they extend up over the hips to help with standing and walking. If HKAFO's are not enough, or if you have hip flexion contractures that make it hard for you to stand and walk, you may need **long leg braces with trunk support,** or **THKAFO**'s. These braces support your trunk with a chest strap that keeps you from bending forward at the hips. Because both of these braces are big and heavy and take a lot of energy to use, most people who use long leg braces with a waist band or with trunk support stand and walk only for exercise.

GUIDELINES FOR INCREASING BRACE TOLERANCE

Because you have spina bifida, you may not be able to feel when your braces rub sore spots on your skin. If you are not careful, you may not notice a pressure sore until it is so deep that your bone breaks down, too. Even small pressure sores can take a long time to heal. Deep pressure sores and sores that hurt bone can take months to heal, and may even need surgery.

When you get new braces, wear them for only 45 to 60 minutes the first time. Then, take them off and look *carefully* at your skin for any red spots.

- ◎ If the redness lasts **longer than 30 minutes**, don't wear the braces until the redness has faded. The next time, wear them for only 20 to 30 minutes. Only increase how long you wear the braces if the redness fades within 30 minutes.
- ◎ If the redness lasts **less than 30 minutes,** increase how long you wear the braces to one and a half to two hours. As long as you don't have red spots that last longer than 30 minutes, continue to increase how long you wear the braces by an hour…until you are wearing them all day!

New braces aren't the only cause of pressure sores. As you change and grow, your feet and legs may not fit properly into your braces. This can cause pressure sores, too. Make sure you look carefully at your feet and legs once a day to make sure that there are no new red spots. Call your physical therapist, doctor, or orthotist if you have problems with redness or sores or if your braces are not fitting properly.

Wheelchairs

Walking may be slow for you or take a lot of energy. As you get older, you may decide that you want to use your energy for something besides walking—like learning in school or shopping with friends. Walking is still important, but getting around faster and easier is important, too. You may decide you want to use a wheelchair. This does not mean that you have given up on walking. It means that you have reached your walking potential and need a more practical way of getting around.

A wheelchair is probably the most important tool you will use to go places. When you choose a wheelchair, you will get a chair that is custom made just for you. So, you need to consider YOU! Where do you live? Where do you go to school and work? How do you usually get places? Answering the following questions will help you decide what wheelchair will best fit your needs.

YOUR HOUSE

- ◎ Does your house have steps to the front door?
- ◎ Are there uneven surfaces around your home, like a gravel driveway or bumpy path?
- ◎ Do you have to go upstairs to get to your bedroom or to a bathroom?
- ◎ How wide are the doorways into your house, into your bedroom, and into the bathroom?
- ◎ How wide are the hallways?
- ◎ How much space is there for you to move between furniture?
- ◎ How much space is there for you to maneuver the wheelchair in the bathroom?

If your house is not completely accessible, instead of making a wheelchair fit into an impossible space, you may want to make the space fit your wheelchair. Many residential improvements, including ramps, can be reported to the Internal Revenue Service (IRS) as medical deductions. To find out more about what qualifies as a deduction, call the local IRS office. You can find their number in the White Pages under "United States Government."

YOUR SCHOOL, JOB, AND ACTIVITIES:

◎ What activities do you do for your job?
◎ Do you need special equipment in order to do your job?
◎ What kind of space do you have to do your work in school and in your job?
◎ Are the bathrooms at school and at work accessible to you?
◎ Do you need to transfer a certain way out of your wheelchair in order to use the toilet?
◎ Do you participate in sports or other activities?

YOUR CAR:

◎ What vehicle will you use for transportation? A van? A big car? A small car? A car with a big trunk?

Once you have looked at where you live, where you go to school or work, and how you usually get places, then you can consider what kind of wheelchair is best for you. **BUT,** before you go to a store to pick one out, **call your doctor.** Let him know that you need a wheelchair and that you are  ready to start looking for one that best suits you. Ask him about possible surgeries that may affect how you fit in your wheelchair. Also ask if he has concerns about the kind of wheelchair you want. Listen to him! Ultimately, your doctor has the final word when he provides a wheelchair prescription.

Call your insurance company to find out how much they will pay for a wheelchair, how often they will pay for new wheelchairs, and how much they will pay for wheelchair repairs.

Call your occupational or physical therapist. She will help solve problems you might have with how you sit, how you propel, and how you get in and out of your wheelchair.

Finally, **choose a wheelchair vendor.** Ask your therapist, clinic, or another satisfied customer for the name of a dependable vendor who will provide you with an appropriate wheelchair and who will give you good service for wheelchair repairs you will need later. Many insurance companies will only pay for wheelchairs provided through their list of vendors. Make sure the vendor you choose is on this list.

DON'T DO IT ALONE! The more people involved, the more likely you will be satisfied with your wheelchair. Your parents, your teacher, and your therapist are all appropriate people to ask to be on your wheelchair team. Can you think of anyone else who might be able to help? There are many wheelchairs from which to choose. The more people on your team, the better.

TYPES OF WHEELCHAIRS AND WHEELCHAIR FEATURES

Frames

Wheelchairs have two basic types of frames. A wheelchair with a **cross frame** will fold flat. It has many moving joints, however, so part of the energy you use to propel the wheels gets lost in the "wiggle" of the frame. A wheelchair with a **rigid frame** has few moving joints. This means most of the energy used when you push the wheels is energy that moves the wheelchair. Unlike a cross frame, a rigid frame does not fold flat. Instead, the wheels come off and the back folds down into a compact box that fits easily into the back seat of a car or into a roomy trunk.

A rigid frame is the frame of choice for people involved in high-performance activities like wheelchair sports. People with limited arm strength or poor endurance for pushing long distances may also benefit from a rigid frame. Finally, wheelchairs tend to break at their moving joints. Because a rigid frame has few moving joints, it is stronger, needs less maintenance, and lasts longer than a cross frame. A rigid frame clearly has many performance advantages over a cross frame. But some people prefer the transportability of a cross frame that folds flat.

"My wheelchair definitely makes my life easier. I wish I could walk, but if I still had crutches and braces I wouldn't be able to do what I can do today!"—K.C.

Wheels

It won't matter what frame you choose if you can't easily reach and propel the wheels. Your choice of wheels will be important in determining how well you can move and maneuver your wheelchair. First, choose a frame that will allow a variety of wheel positions. A forward wheel position will give you the "tippiness" you need to do wheelies to maneuver curbs and stairs by yourself. This slightly forward position also puts the wheels in a better place for your arms to reach and propel the wheelchair easily.

If you can't control a tippy wheelchair, position the wheels slightly rearward on the frame. Then, make an appointment with your therapist to practice the skills you need for wheelies. Without this important skill, you can't go out without someone to help you over potential obstacles. As a growing young person, it is important for you to be able to do things and go places by yourself.

While **solid wheels** are more efficient on smooth surfaces, **pneumatic**, or air-filled, tires perform better on rough or uneven surfaces. Most people have to propel their wheelchairs over both smooth and rough surfaces, such as grass, asphalt, and carpet. Pneumatic wheels are therefore usually the best choice. Maintaining air-filled tires can be as easy as buying a tube patch kit or a new tire tube at a bicycle shop. A wheelchair with flat tires is hard to push. If you think you will have trouble keeping your tires properly filled, consider getting solid wheels.

The small front wheels on your wheelchair are called **casters.** Like the bigger rear wheels, solid casters work better on smooth surfaces, while pneumatic casters work better on rough surfaces. The smaller the caster, the better your wheelchair will respond to steering. But, small wheels tend to get stuck on very rough surfaces such as gravel or soft ground. Discuss with your therapist and vendor what kind of casters would be best for your activities and for the surfaces around your home and community.

Seats

Many people with spina bifida have muscle imbalance, poor sensation, and scoliosis. This makes finding the best wheelchair seat essential. The right seat can help prevent and manage pressure sores and muscle contractures.

It is most important that the back, seat, and footrests support your hips, knees, and ankles at right angles. A standard sling seat and back are generally not recommended. Instead, a contour or solid cushioned seat and back are encouraged to provide adequate postural support, accommodations for scoliosis, and pressure relief. Both ETAC and Quickie make a contour seat and back with a velcro strap system that provides adequate support with minimal extra hardware.

Your seat should be long enough to support your thighs but short enough that you can stick two fingers width-wise between the front end of the seat and the back of your legs. Your wheelchair back should be high enough to support your back, but low enough to allow you to turn and reach into a bag on the back of your chair. The lower the back, the more you can move and use your arms and shoulders. If your sitting balance is good, the back of your wheelchair should stop just below your shoulder blades.

Cushions

What kind of wheelchair cushion should you put in your seat? If you have never had a pressure sore, a standard foam pressure relief cushion may be all you need. If you have had a pressure sore, are overweight, or don't move much in the chair, a more adequate pressure-relieving cushion is necessary.

One cushion often recommended for adolescent wheelchair users is the ROHO cushion. The ROHO cushion has air-filled, balloon-like cells. A flat ROHO is like having no pressure-relieving cushion at all. If you think you may have trouble keeping a ROHO cushion properly inflated, ask your therapist and vendor about other cushion options.

Finally, a variety of cushions are available for people who have problems with incontinence. Most of these cushions have machine-washable covers and a waterproof layer protecting the pressure-relieving foam. Ask your therapist or vendor to discuss these with you.

ESSENTIAL WHEELCHAIR SKILLS

Can you transfer to and from your wheelchair from your bed or from a chair? If you fall out of your wheelchair, can you get back in by yourself? Can you do wheelies to get up and down curbs and stairs? Lateral transfers, transfers from the floor to your wheelchair, and wheelies are **WHEELCHAIR SKILLS YOU CAN'T DO WITHOUT!** As long as you have these skills, you can go anywhere and do anything. If you have trouble with any of these skills, make an appointment with your therapist and practice, *practice,* **PRACTICE!**

Driving

"I want to drive!!!"

If one of your goals is to drive, consider contacting a driver's education program for people with special needs. These programs are usually offered through a local city hospital and can be found in the Yellow Pages under "Driver's Education." Step by step, an adapted driver's education program will equip you to drive.

The first step is a driver evaluation. During this evaluation, someone will closely look at your strength, range of motion, vision, and reaction time. You may also take a standard written driver's test. Some states require that you take the classroom and driving education from the same place. If the program does not offer basic classroom training, you may need to contact the Bureau of Motor

Vehicles to find out how you can meet their requirements while still getting the special service you need.

Most people with spina bifida have the physical ability to drive with adequate adaptations. Some people, however, have visual perceptual problems that can make driving dangerous. Although driving may be important to you, it is possible that you may have to give up on this goal. You will find out during your driver evaluation whether driving is feasible for you.

Next, an engineer will help determine what special equipment you need to effectively steer, brake, accelerate, activate all secondary controls, and maintain sitting balance. For example, instead of foot pedals for the brakes and accelerator, you may need hand-operated controls. The program will provide a properly equipped vehicle for you to learn on. Once you get your license, the program will help you to obtain modifications to your own van or car. Vocational rehabilitation may pay for these modifications. After your car has been modified, someone will check to ensure that the work has been done with no obvious mistakes.

If you want to drive when you turn sixteen, start the process early. Make sure driving is included as a goal on your transition plan when you turn fourteen.

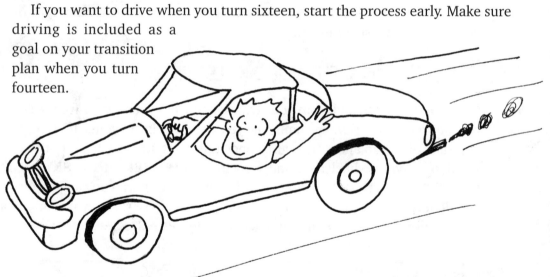

Vacation Planning and Travel

Whether you want to have a fun weekend away from home or a satisfying trip around the country, the most important step is to **PLAN**. Make an itinerary of where and when you plan to go places. Call the Chamber of Commerce in the cities which you plan to visit to get information about attractions, lodging, and activities that are handicap accessible. Call the hotels where you plan to stay to reserve a wheelchair accessible room. Ask the airline, train, or bus company what kind of arrangements they make for transporting your wheelchair or walker. Does this service require an extra charge?

Consider asking someone to be your traveling companion and helper. If you don't have a traveling companion, call the airline, train, or bus company to confirm that someone will be expecting you to assist you with your luggage if necessary. You may be able to modify a wheeled suitcase to sling over the back of your wheelchair so you can pull it behind you.

Make a list of everything you will need to pack in your suitcase and in your carry-on bag. What do you need to have in your carry-on bag in case your luggage is lost or delayed? You have many things to remember to ensure a foolproof vacation, but if you just remember to **plan thoroughly**, you'll have few surprises. Good luck!

TRAVEL RESOURCES

"Access Travel: Airports"

Cost: Free
Write the Federal Aviation Administration,
U.S. Department of Transportation,
Washington, DC 20591

"Access Amtrak"

Write the Office of Customer Relations,
Amtrak,
P.O. Box 2709
Washington, DC 20013

Bus Lines

Call the bus companies and ask for staff from Greyhound's "Helping
    Hand Service" or Trailways' "Good Samaritan Plan"
Greyhound Contact: Helping Hand Service for the Handicapped
Greyhound Lines
Greyhound Towers
Phoenix, AZ 85077

Renting a car with hand controls

Avis (1-800-331-1212)
National Car Rentals (1-800-328-4567)

Travelling Like Everybody Else. Jacqueline Freedman. New York: Adama Books, 1987.

Conclusion

Now you can go...with crutches, a walker, braces, or a wheelchair. You can drive...to a football game or to the mall! You can plan a trip and travel around the country. You have choices about when and how to go. So go, GO, GO!

PART TWO

. . . .

Relationships

. . . .

(7)

Great Expectations

(Relationships and Developing Independence)

Sharon Sellet, B.S.

A relationship is a connection between people. You have relationships with your parents, brothers and sisters, friends at school, teachers, the people who help you with your health care, and even the delivery man. Some relationships are with casual acquaintances. Others involve deep feelings that may develop over a long period of time.

Your relationships will come and go depending on your life experiences. Relationships with your parents and cousins are pretty automatic and will last a long time. They require ordinary care such as respect and co-operation and communication. The same is true of relationships you form at school or work. These are the relationships you develop with the people you see every day. Relationships grow just like plants. They start small and can develop into real friendships. The more relationships you develop, the greater the chance for friendships. Just like making strawberry shortcake. You don't just pick one strawberry. You pick a whole basketful, because not every strawberry is shortcake quality. Relationships are the same way—you need to develop lots of relationships to cultivate a friendship.

This chapter offers tips on turning relationships into friendships. It also suggest ways to troubleshoot problems with relationships *outside* of your family. (The next chapter discusses problems with relationships *inside* your family.)

Building Friendships

Making and keeping friends is easier for some people than for others. You may think that because of spina bifida and some of your difficulties and extra equipment that you may have a harder time making friends. That isn't necessarily so. The biggest limit anyone has is their attitude. You can't really do anything about having spina bifida, but you can control your attitude about it. People will pick up on your attitude. If you act like you're a pitiful loser because you have spina bifida, people won't want to be around you. If you have high self-esteem, you will feel more confident and sure of yourself. Most likely you will be someone who makes friends easily. Spina bifida is only a part of who you are, so be proud of what you have accomplished. You are a person first who just happens to have a condition known as spina bifida.

3 Friendship Facts

1. Everyone wants to have friends.
2. The best way to make friends is to be one.
3. Friendships are give and take.

ESSENTIAL SOCIAL SKILLS

People who always seem to have a lot of friends and things to do are usually called popular. How did they get that way? People are not born popular. They have learned the social skills of making friends. Skills used in social situations are learned and developed with experience and practice. These are complex and subtle ways of behaving, communicating, and responding to people. Social skills can be learned through *observation, awareness,* and *problem solving.*

Observation

Through observation, you watch how other people handle situations that are hard for you. For example, you may see friends get teased and embarrassed and notice that they don't let it bother them. They smile and laugh with the person who made the remark rather than becoming angry and hurt. Or you may observe how a popular classmate enters into a group and starts a conversation. He or she might look directly at someone in the group with a friendly "Hi!" or "What's up?" Imagine yourself starting a conversation or handling teasing in a similar situation.

Awareness

Awareness means noticing the "cues" that others give you. These are like clues that give you a hint of something. Mothers are very good at giving cues to their children when they want them to behave in a certain way. The cue might be a stern look when children are giggling in church or "Quiet!" whispered in a serious voice.

To make and keep friendships, you need to know how to both send cues and to read or interpret cues.

Interpreting Cues. Interpreting cues means watching for a change in facial expressions, listening for a change in someone's tone of voice, or paying attention to body language. For instance, Randy kept talking to his friend, Tim, after the movie started. Tim did not look at Randy, nor did he answer. The clue, or cue, was that it was not the appropriate time for conversation. Tim continued to ignore Randy's comments so Randy would get the clue to be quiet.

Sending Cues. When you send a cue, you use your own voice or body language to help get your message across. For example, Becky complained that no one ever stopped to talk with her at lunch. Her counselor observed that Becky, who uses a wheelchair, always looked down when someone talked to her or when she said something. Looking down and not directly at the person you are addressing makes it hard for the person to "read" your expressions. Becky produced a more "inviting" look by holding her head up high and looking directly into people's eyes when she spoke.

Joining in the Conversation. Observation and awareness are important in keeping up with conversations. People often talk and move on to new subjects rather quickly. Conversational skills require listening for new thoughts and opinions and responding appropriately to what is said. Some techniques for entering a conversation include:

- ◎ Listen for important ideas to talk about.
- ◎ Respond to someone's comment.
- ◎ Ask a question and share opinions.
- ◎ Give a compliment.
- ◎ Make eye contact.

You can find interesting things to talk about in books, newspapers, magazines, and the Internet. Why not pick a hobby or something that interests you and become an expert?

Problem Solving for Embarrassing Situations

Being able to handle embarrassment is another skill that is very important in social situations. Everyone gets embarrassed at one time or another during school, work, or social activities. Most embarrassing situations can be handled with a smile or some humor. You can plan for these situations by thinking of some really horrible, embarrassing moment and imagining ways you would respond. For example, what if your wheelchair tire went flat during the awards banquet? What would be a good way to handle it? Think of the words you would use and even something humorous to say about it.

Rehearsing or role playing difficult situations is a great way to prepare for embarrassing circumstances or ones that make you uncomfortable.

Think of at least two solutions to the following situations:

The "What If" Game

What If . . . I dropped my tray in the cafeteria?

What If . . . I'm not picked (or picked last) for the relay team in gym class?

What If . . . I left my homework on the kitchen table *again?*

What If . . . My clothes got wet?

Managers in business or executives are always playing the **"What If"** game and coming up with new solutions to problems or new products. They have developed the skill of *thinking ahead* and *problem solving*. This is why they are the executives.

People with spina bifida are also *managers* because of all the planning it takes to coordinate and manage their health care. You have to plan ahead to make sure you have the equipment you need for hygiene and a bathroom with enough room to maneuver. (For specific tips on handling embarrassment related to these issues, be sure to check Chapter 5.) Likewise, you need to know where the accessible entrances are, arrange for the kind of transportation you need, and be prepared for appointments. These are personal life skills to work on and develop. Being a good manager will also help you to be out and living on your own.

Teasing and Personal Questions.
A special source of embarrassment for many young people with spina bifida is dealing with teasing and personal questions. Teasing can be friendly and affectionate—a way to express feelings and bond some friendships. But teasing can also be stinging and humiliating. Likewise, questions about spina bifida, other difficulties, or equipment you use may be well-intentioned and aimed at getting to know you better. But questions can also be tactless, intrusive, and personal. If you are being teased or questioned and it is uncomfortable and hurtful, you can do a couple of things:

1. Toughen up and let the teasing roll off your back. Look the teaser in the eye and completely ignore the comment. Deep down inside, you know anyone who teases destructively is a bully with a poor self-image.

2. If you feel like you must say something, try:
   ◎ "Back off and leave me alone."
   ◎ "This is my concern and not yours."
You don't want to be pulled into a verbal fight. Just deliver a comeback and go on with your activity.

3. To deal with intrusive remarks, think of the questions or comments that bother you the most and plan for your response. Examples:
   ◎ "This is not a topic I care to discuss with you."
   ◎ "I use a wheelchair to get from here to there."
   ◎ "I was born with spina bifida and my legs work differently."

Don't Wait for Others to Make the First Move

Some people see differences in others as barriers to friendship. They may not think a person using a wheelchair is able to participate in activities or go places that people who walk unassisted can go. You can't change the way people think, but you can *show* them the part of you that is similar to them. Developing common interests or hobbies allows you to be a person who is interesting and participates in activities.

Having a variety of experiences and activities creates more opportunities for friendships. Participating in school clubs or community groups increases the number of people you meet and gives you a common goal to work on. Schools and neighborhoods have youth clubs or teen councils that need people to make phone calls, plan meetings, and participate in the activities. Service clubs and church groups are also great places to meet people and focus on a project.

A lot happens when two people work together on a project. They:

- ◎ Meet and talk with new people
- ◎ Share a goal
- ◎ Feel good about accomplishing something.

The fact that you use a wheelchair, walker, or braces becomes less important because your ideas and interests are what describe you.

8

Family Matters

Sharon Sellet, B.S.

Brothers and Sisters

Brothers and sisters have very special relationships. Sometimes they are very close to each other emotionally and share bedrooms, clothes, secrets, and snacks. Just as often, they go through periods of disliking each other and arguing over space, clothes, chores, and snacks. These are ordinary and usual feelings for brothers and sisters (siblings) to have.

You probably can remember times when you were doubling up with laughter with your sister or brother one day, and loudly arguing the next, or even 15 minutes later. That's the way sibling relationships usually are.

What makes any of this different for you and your siblings (brothers/sisters) is the way spina bifida can complicate your life and your relationships. As you know better than anyone, spina bifida makes your life different in some ways. If you have had surgeries, or another complication such as broken bones or pressure sores, it very likely disrupted your brothers' and sisters' lives also. Perhaps your parents had to miss an important event of your brothers'/sisters' because of the medical necessity in your life. Or perhaps your parents had to decide between buying a new wheelchair for you or taking everyone on a family vacation. Perhaps your brother didn't get to go on that camping trip because you had emergency surgery.

You know that having medical procedures and waiting for appointments is not fun. Your siblings know that it might not be fun, but they also know that everyone rallies around you and brings special treats and spends time visiting. It may also seem that these times often happen when THEY have a special event or game. Then Mom and Dad have to miss it and THEY even have to find their own rides to the special event. Your brothers and sisters end up feeling like LIFE'S NOT FAIR. You have probably felt this way too.

Your brothers or sisters may also feel other emotions that complicate your relationship with them. Perhaps they feel angry because their lives were put on hold while your special medical needs were tended to. And then they feel guilty about feeling angry. Or perhaps they are sometimes embarrassed to be seen with a brother or sister who uses a wheelchair or walker. They may even feel as if they need to be "extra good" so your parents won't have as much to worry about.

If your brothers or sisters are older, they may have been called on to help with your care—catheterization, bracing, appointments, transportation. Some brothers and sisters of kids with spina bifida have said this is too much responsibility. They felt like parents and were even scared sometimes. They especially didn't like being called on to help with the care without being included in the decisions. Sometimes moms and dads forget that brothers and sisters want to learn about spina bifida and have questions.

How do you think your brothers and sisters would describe you? Like M.B.: *"Sometimes spoiled with too much attention"*? Or like B.K.A.: *"Outgoing and social"*? Or perhaps a combination of positive and negative characteristics?

Some actual reactions and observations of brothers/sisters of kids with spina bifida are . . .

◎ I was scared because I never really knew everything about all the surgeries. I had to help take care of my sister, but no one asked me what I thought.

◎ People give him things just because he's in a wheelchair.

◎ We get good parking places!

◎ I wish everyone had a brother with spina bifida.
◎ I felt like I was her mother. I had too much responsibility.
◎ We've gone to conferences in places we probably wouldn't have visited otherwise.
◎ Sometimes it's embarrassing because my brother acts weird and he might have a bladder or bowel accident.
◎ We went to Disneyland and didn't have to wait in lines and got to ride longer.

Some concerns of brothers and sisters are . . .

◎ They will have to take care of the brother/sister with spina bifida.
◎ They feel guilty if they get to do something that their brother/sister with spina bifida can't do.
◎ They think parents have different expectations of the child with spina bifida.
◎ Sometimes parents don't think the child with spina bifida can do certain chores or get certain things, so they (parents) make the siblings do it.
◎ The brother or sister with spina bifida gets punished less.

What to Do?

Of course, it is not your fault that you have spina bifida. You would probably give anything to be just a regular kid—to get the same amount of attention from your parents as your siblings do and to do the same things (including chores) that other kids do.

Still, it is important to realize that spina bifida affects everyone in your family, not just you. There are probably things that both you and your brothers and sisters can do to reduce that impact and to improve your relationship. Here are some suggestions:

RESPECT EACH OTHER'S INTERESTS

Everyone is different and will have different experiences, according to their abilities. In typical families, brothers and sisters, brothers and brothers, sisters and sisters may all develop very different interests. Perhaps Michael excels at all sports and is a star basketball player. Lee may like video games and scary movies and spend lots of time on the computer writing short stories. Kelly may love animals, take care of all the neighborhood strays, and dream of being a veterinarian. You don't have to share your siblings' interests, but it's nice to learn something about them and get a taste of what interests your brother or sister about them. Showing that you care about what interests your siblings shows that you care about *them*. Knowing their interests gives you something to talk about. You may even find that you like what they like and can share some enjoyable times together.

Besides respecting different interests, you and your family need to understand that you each have different ways of doing things. Certain things may be more difficult for you, but your siblings may not understand why. They may need you to explain why you "hog" the bathroom so long in the morning or why you need to practice walking with braces sometimes instead of speeding things up and using your wheelchair. And you shouldn't assume that everything is easy for your siblings just because they don't have spina bifida. They might be shy and have trouble making friends. Or maybe they have trouble focusing their attention when they're doing their homework and need to have the CD player turned off. You may like to keep the window in your bedroom open, and your brother may like to keep it shut.

Understanding and respecting differences is an important social skill to have. You have to be aware when your differences affect someone else and be prepared to work out a compromise. You shouldn't always have to have it your way, and neither should your brothers/sisters.

SHARE YOUR FEELINGS

Families share a lot of emotions together. They get angry at each other, they get excited and happy, they experience sadness and jealousy and even fear. The best way for these feelings to be recognized is to share them with people who are important—parents, brothers/sisters, friends, or even teachers and counselors. Talking about your concerns or feelings will help make them manageable.

You and your siblings can learn a lot about each other if you share your feelings. You can turn potential misunderstandings into understandings, give each other support when you need it, and let off steam in a healthy way! If you *don't* share your feelings, people have to guess at the reason for your moods and can come to the wrong conclusion.

Try to make a habit of talking to your brother/sister about what is happening with you. For example:

- ◎ I felt mad when the lift stopped working and I got stuck on the bus.
- ◎ It was neat being interviewed by the school paper.
- ◎ I'm afraid the doctor might say I need surgery.

Don't shy away from telling your siblings your feelings about them—good or bad. If it hurt your feelings when your sister acted like she didn't know you at school, or if you're annoyed that she moved your wheelchair away from the bed where you can't reach it, or if you're happy she invited you to the movies, tell her!

There are ways to tell your siblings you're upset that will help everyone keep their cool. Use "I" statements describing your feelings, rather than "you" statements. Say: "I felt sad when you didn't say "hi" back to me in the hall. My friends saw you ignore me and I was really embarrassed." Not: "You made me so upset when you ignored me in the hall. You made me look like a fool in front of my friends." Another good way to communicate feelings is to begin by acknowledging that you understand why your sibling did something. For example, "I know there's not much space between our beds, but when you put my wheelchair by the door, I have to crawl over there. It's not a fun way to start the day." If you model a polite and open way of discussing feelings, your siblings may do the same, and family life will be pleasanter for everyone.

LET SIBLINGS KNOW YOU CARE

Find out what is going on in your brothers' and sisters' lives. Ask questions, be interested, concerned, and supportive if they have disappointments. Say:

- ◎ "I'm sorry you got cut from the team."
- ◎ "Where is your club going backpacking next summer?"
- ◎ "Doesn't it hurt when you get tackled?"

This lets them know that you think their hopes, dreams, and needs are as important as yours, even though your special needs are sometimes the focus of family attention.

SHOW YOUR APPRECIATION

Be appreciative of the small and large things your brothers or sisters do for you and SHOW it. Say, "Thanks for bringing my book bag into the house." Or "If you'll drop me off at the movies, I'll bring in the garbage cans for you next Monday." If you acknowledge their help, they will be more likely to do it again in the future.

Do Things Yourself

Everybody benefits when you learn to do things for yourself. You learn skills that will help you live on your own some day. The more you can do for yourself, the more capable and competent you feel. As your skills grow, you can take over chores or other responsibilities that your brothers and sisters were handling. When responsibilities are shared fairly, everybody feels like an equal and contributing member of the family. Nobody is seen as the "favorite," and there is bound to be less friction.

Perhaps you and your family can discuss a fair way of dividing up the chores. Perhaps your family might decide that each kid should have the same number of weekly chores. Or that everyone should spend about the same amount of time per week doing chores. You may not be able to mow the yard each week, but you can unload the dishwasher and clean the sink and toilet. You can ask your siblings or parents to teach you to do the laundry or other chores that will help you become more independent.

Brothers and sisters will be around for a long time. Treat them like good friends. Be interested in their activities and be respectful of their time with friends. Expect them to do the same with you. Develop interests you can share, such as music, movies, games, sports, or hobbies. Learn to stay out of each others' way, but actively look for ways to support each other.

Life's Not Fair

Most likely, everyone in the family feels that life is not fair from time to time. Your mom may feel as if she is always doing the laundry while everyone else is watching their favorite TV show. You may feel left out because your brothers went on a hiking trip. Your sister feels cheated because her birthday celebration was wedged between the "big games" and a P.T.A. meeting. The point is, everyone has disappointments and feelings of "not fair" in families.

It's perfectly normal to sometimes feel down, or as if life's not fair. It's normal, that is, as long as you are able to look at the bright side of things again before too long. It's not healthy to feel sad or angry or depressed *all* the time.

If you feel so miserable that you don't want to do anything, be with anyone, or take care of your appearance, it's time to get help. If you have an IEP, there may be a social worker or psychologist on your team you can talk with. A favorite teacher or school counselor may also be able to point you in the right direction. In addition, you may find it helpful to meet and share your feelings with other young people who have spina bifida. They may be able to give you practical tips on coping with specific problems. Just as importantly, you may get a boost out of learning that there are others in the same boat who have weathered similar storms.

You can make contact with other people with spina bifida by going to a spina bifida clinic to meet other people your age. Or you can contact the Spina Bifida Association of America. Write or call the Spina Bifida Association of America and ask about upcoming conferences or about putting you in touch with a support group or pen pal. The address is:

Spina Bifida Association of America
4590 MacArthur Blvd., N.W., Suite 250
Washington, DC 20007-4226
Phone: 1-800-621-3141

Intimate Details

(Sexuality Issues)

Marlene Lutkenhoff, R.N., M.S.N.

The ability to love and be loved does not change when a person has a disability. You are a sexual being and you have the right to express your sexuality. The challenge lies in discovering and accepting your own sexuality so that you feel free to share yourself with others. The questions and answers that follow will help you think about what you know and how you feel about your own sexuality.

General Questions

Where can I go for information about the male or female anatomy?

- ◎ Your parents
- ◎ Your doctor or nurse
- ◎ The library—check out a basic anatomy and physiology book. It will have a chapter on the reproductive organs.

What's a "period"?

A period refers to menstruation. Menstruation is normal in females and occurs roughly from the ages of 10 to 50 in women who are not pregnant.

As you may know, blood builds up on the walls of the uterus every month to prepare for a possible pregnancy. If a pregnancy does not occur, the blood is released through the vagina. This release of blood is known as menstruation and usually lasts about five days. During this time, women wear sanitary pads or tampons to protect their clothes. Some women with spina bifida who already wear disposable undergarments may not feel that they need additional protection. If pads or tampons are used, they need to be changed about every three to four hours. If you can catheterize yourself, you should have no trouble inserting a tampon into the vagina. Some women put K-Y Jelly on the tampon to make it slide in easier.

When they are menstruating, women with spina bifida may or may not experience cramps (painful muscle spasms in the uterus and/or abdomen). No one need know you are having your period, especially if you are extra careful with keeping yourself clean.

What is a wet dream?

A wet dream is a normal occurrence for many teenage boys and men during sleep. When this happens, the penis becomes hard, and sperm is released. Males with spina bifida may not experience wet dreams if the nerves involved are not functioning.

What if someone wants to touch my private parts?

No one has the right to touch you without your permission. Sometimes doctors and nurses need to examine you or perform a procedure that requires them to see or touch your private parts. When they do so, they should respect your need for privacy by covering you appropriately and shutting the door. They should also explain to you exactly what they are doing and why they need to do it. Don't be afraid to ask questions.

When should a girl begin to see a gynecologist?

A gynecologist is a doctor who specializes in problems specific to women. A girl should begin seeing one by age 18, or sooner if she is sexually active or has female-type problems such as irregular periods, too much menstrual flow, or missed periods. During your first visit, the gynecologist will do a pelvic exam, as described below.

What is a pelvic exam?

A pelvic exam involves inserting an instrument into the vagina so that the gynecologist can be sure that there are no problems. The gynecologist will do a pap smear by scraping off a sample of cervical tissue to look for signs of cancer or other problems. The cervix is the end of the uterus and is the passageway from the uterus to the vagina. It looks like a small donut and feels soft like the tip of your nose. The gynecologist will also feel your abdomen to make sure your ovaries, etc., are the right size and in the right place.

Positioning for a pelvic exam may be difficult for a woman with spina bifida. Usually your legs need to be spread apart for the doctor to examine you. You and the doctor will have to find out what position works for you. A pelvic exam may be a little uncomfortable, but it should not hurt. Be sure the care provider wears latex-free gloves.

Dating Questions

How do I know if I'm sexually attractive?

People who accept themselves and feel comfortable with themselves are generally attractive. When people like who they are, they want to look their best by keeping clean and wearing clothes that look good on them. Don't let your weight, or braces, or wheelchair be excuses. Make the best of what you have.

Why does it seem so hard to make friends sometimes?

Disabilities can sometimes scare people. It may be up to you to make the first move. Act friendly and interested in people. Stay informed about a variety of subjects so you are interesting to be around. Join groups and activities where you can meet people. Go out and enjoy yourself.

What if no one asks me out?

Consider going by yourself or asking someone you like to go with you. Remember, don't be afraid to make the first move. All relationships involve a little risk-taking. Remember that people without disabilities have lots of dating-type problems too.

What if my date wants to know about my disability?

Tell him or her whatever you're comfortable sharing. This book will help you understand your disability so that you can explain it to others. Always be upfront and honest. Whether you are dating someone with or without a disability, it is important for both of you to be able to express your feelings openly. The longer you date someone, the easier and more important it becomes to share feelings. Accepting each other emotionally is more important than accepting one or the other's disability.

What if I'm with my date and I pass gas, or have a bowel or bladder accident?

Be prepared for that possibility. Think of what you'll say before it happens. Take care of your toileting needs before you go out and hopefully everything will go smoothly. But if it doesn't, excuse yourself, clean yourself up, and go on.

What if I feel like having sex, but know it's not the right time for me or my partner?

Deciding to have sexual intercourse with someone is a big step. Making that decision has a lot to do with a person's values and upbringing. If the time is not right for you, it may take a lot of self-control on your part to wait. If the time is not right for your partner, you must respect his or her decision. It's okay to feel like having sex, but don't have sex for the wrong reasons—such as because of a need to feel masculine or a need to feel wanted.

"Dating relationships are the part of my life the most affected by spina bifida." - E.B.

What if my friends are all having sex?

If all your friends say they're having sex, probably some of them are exaggerating. Never do something just because your friends might be doing it. That's peer pressure. Remember, they may just be bragging.

How can you tell if you're in love?

Mature love occurs in a relationship that develops slowly, over time. It means caring deeply about someone else. When you are with that person, you are happy. You enjoy doing things together and sharing your thoughts about everything and anything. There is trust and understanding between you.

Sexual Intercourse Questions

What is the most important organ involved in sexual intercourse?

The brain. This organ tells us what we feel and think.

What exactly is sexual intercourse?

It is an expression of physical love between two people. It includes kissing and touching and usually involves the male's penis being inserted into the female's vagina.

If I don't have genital sensation, can I still enjoy sexual intercourse?

Yes. Many people find that other parts of their body will make up for the lack of sensation in their genitals.

Can a male with spina bifida have an erection?

Possibly. The more sensation you have in your legs, the more chance you have of having an erection.

If I can't have an erection, how do I have sexual intercourse?

There are erection aids that are available to help people have an erection. Your family physician or urologist should be able to help you in this area. A urologist is a doctor who specializes in the care of the urinary system, including the bladder and kidneys.

Can a male with spina bifida ejaculate?

Most males with spina bifida cannot ejaculate—release sperm through the penis. Those who can have a very low back lesion.

What is an orgasm?

An orgasm is basically a strong sensation that occurs during intercourse or stimulation of the genitals. It feels good and is accompanied by several genital contractions.

What if I don't have an orgasm during sexual intercourse?

That's okay. Many people do not experience an orgasm every time they have sexual intercourse. It is not needed in order for you to enjoy sexual intercourse. Being physically and emotionally close feels good, too.

If my legs won't bend and I can't control them, what position is good for sexual intercourse?

Only you and your partner can decide that by trying different positions until one feels right for you. There is no one right position. Whatever is comfortable for you and your partner is okay.

What is lubrication?

When women become sexually excited, they get moist (lubricate) in and around the vagina. This makes it easier for a man to insert his penis. Lubrication often does not occur in females with spina bifida. Women with spina bifida can use K-Y Jelly in place of lubrication by inserting some in the vagina with a finger and placing some on the man's penis. Males with spina bifida should also use K-Y Jelly on their penis during intercourse to avoid irritation. It needs to be reapplied frequently.

How can I avoid a bladder or bowel accident during intercourse?

You might not be able to, but a good way to try is to catheterize your bladder and do your bowel program before sexual intercourse.

Pregnancy Questions

When is a woman most likely to get pregnant?

You are most likely to get pregnant roughly halfway into your menstrual cycle. A menstrual cycle is calculated by counting how many days there are between the first day you menstruate one month and the first day you menstruate the next month. (You count the first day you menstruate as day one.) Many women's menstrual cycles last about 28 days, so tend to occur about the same time every month. This means they are most likely to get pregnant 14 days after the start of their last menstrual period. This is when they release an egg (ovulate).

If your cycle is shorter or longer than 28 days, count the number of days and then divide that number in half. For example, if your cycle usually lasts 20 days, you are most likely to get pregnant on the tenth day of your cycle.

Egg and sperm can live about 48 to 72 hours. If you want to avoid pregnancy, this means you will need to take special precaution two to three days before and after ovulation. (For a woman with a 28-day cycle, this would mean from day 11 to day 17.) Talk to your health care provider for more information about how this applies to you.

Can a girl become pregnant the first time she has sexual intercourse?

Absolutely.

Can a female with spina bifida get pregnant?

Yes. It is important, though, to plan and discuss a pregnancy with an obstetrician skilled in high risk pregnancies before getting pregnant. This is because medical complications may occur, and your doctor will want to discuss these possibilities with you. It is vital that you receive excellent care before and during your pregnancy. With excellent care, it is quite possible to have a successful pregnancy.

Can a male with spina bifida get a female pregnant?

Guys should not assume they are infertile. If they are able to have an erection and have sexual intercourse, they should take precautions if they don't want a pregnancy to occur.

Men who are unable to ejaculate will probably not be able to impregnate a woman without medical assistance. They may be able to father children through artificial insemination, however. In this procedure, sperm is removed from the male using various devices or stimulation techniques. It is then placed in the woman's vagina or uterus with a slender tube or pipette.

There are tests that can determine whether a male is fertile. The semen (thin milky fluid that is discharged from the penis during an ejaculation) can be examined under a microscope to see if enough mobile sperm are present.

How can pregnancy be prevented?

There are a variety of ways to prevent pregnancies. These include:

- ◎ not having sex during certain times of the month,
- ◎ taking birth control pills,
- ◎ having a Depro Provera® shot, and
- ◎ using condoms

One type of birth control that may be too difficult for you to use is the diaphragm. This is an object that needs to be inserted into the vagina so that it covers the cervix. Be sure anything you use does not contain latex. Talk to your doctor about the best method for you before you become sexually active.

If you are a female with spina bifida and your partner uses a latex condom, be sure he uses a sheepskin condom on top of the latex one. If you are a male with spina bifida, always use a sheepskin condom next to your skin. As explained in Chapter 1, people with spina bifida often have latex allergies. A latex condom must be used in addition to the sheepskin one because latex is the best protective barrier against sexually transmitted diseases.

If my partner or I have spina bifida, will our baby have spina bifida?

You have a good chance of having a baby without spina bifida. However, the chances of having a baby with spina bifida are greater than for someone who does not have spina bifida. Since the risks can vary from individual to individual, you should talk to a genetic counselor. A genetic counselor can help you understand your risk for having a baby with spina bifida, and also determine if there are other genetic risks. Your doctor will be able to refer you to a genetic counselor.

Can I improve my chances of having a healthy baby?

Yes. Several months before you start trying to get pregnant, talk to an obstetrician (a doctor who delivers babies) or your family physician. He or she can prescribe a vitamin called folic acid. It is usually taken daily, at least one month before conceiving and also during the first three months of pregnancy. Research studies show that taking folic acid supplements can significantly reduce the chance of having a baby with spina bifida. Your doctor will be able to talk to you about other ways to have a healthy pregnancy.

If I don't have much sensation below my waist, how will I know I'm in labor?

Your pregnancy would be monitored closely. You would probably need to have your baby by C-section, which means the doctor would make an incision on your abdomen and into the uterus to deliver the baby.

In Conclusion...

You probably still have many questions about your sexuality. There are books that can help answer your questions. Some of these are listed below. You probably also know some people you can confide in. The main thing to remember is don't isolate yourself. Go out and meet people. Keep trying until you find a friend to enjoy life with.

Books

Sexuality and the Person with Spina Bifida, by Stephen Sloan. Washington, DC: Spina Bifida Association. To buy, call 1-800-621-3141 or write to Spina Bifida Association of America, 4590 MacArthur Blvd., N.W., Suite 250, Washington, DC 20007-4226.

What's Happening to Me? The Answers to Some of the World's Most Embarrassing Questions, by Peter Mayle. Secaucus, NJ: Carol Publishing Group. To buy, call 1-800-447-BOOK.

PART THREE

Growing Up

16

Tools & Techniques

(for School and Beyond)

Sharon Sellet, B.S.

Students with spina bifida are not all the same, just as all students in a certain school are not all the same. People are different, and, as you know, some people are better at learning some things than others. You may be very good at remembering words to a song, while a friend may be very good at remembering sports statistics.

Students with spina bifida, like all students, have a wide range of abilities. Some have very little difficulty with school, while others struggle to get decent grades. Most students with spina bifida do share certain similarities in learning that make some parts of school difficult. These have to do with **attention, memory,** and **recalling information (retrieval).** But remember, *all students* have problems with these occasionally.

Most people with spina bifida have differences in their nervous systems which could have an effect on learning. The nervous system is like a computer "main frame" for all your body systems. The nervous system sorts out and sends messages, stores information, and delegates jobs to different parts of your body. People with spina bifida may have differences in any of these functions because of differences in the structure of the spine and brain. (See Chapter 1.) This doesn't mean that you can't be successful in school. It just means that you have to figure out, with some help, what is hard for you, then find ways to get around it.

It's like going places in a wheelchair. If you like to go to a certain store and the entrance has steps, you find out where the accessible entrance is so you can get to where you want to be. For some students, school is like steps into a building. You might need to figure out an alternate way to get to where you want to be.

If you already know what problems you have in school, such as remembering facts for a test, or writing, or grammar, or adding math facts, you have half the battle won. Ask your teacher or tutor if he or she can help you figure out ways to be successful. This might mean learning certain skills like **keyboarding, time management, setting goals, and organizing notes.** It could also mean **speaking up (advocating)** for yourself for the **changes you need (accommodations).** Don't be shy about asking for specific changes that you think would help you. For example:

- ◎ "May I tape record the class?"
- ◎ "Can I be paired with another note taker?"
- ◎ "May I have a copy of the class outline?"
- ◎ "May I take the tests orally?"

Tools for Schoolwork

This section suggests techniques for dealing with four areas of learning that are often difficult for students with spina bifida:

- ◎ Memory
- ◎ Attention
- ◎ Organization
- ◎ Writing

Memory

Memory is like your closet. It stores information like names, ideas, and facts. Then you retrieve (recall) or get that information out when you need it. Some memory is "short term," which means you only need it for a little while. Instructions for making a recipe are short term. Some memory is "long term," which means you keep it forever. Like your friend's telephone number, or the names of your cousins, or the months of the year, or spelling words and math facts. These are the things that you need to get out of your "memory closet" over and over again.

In school, you need to use both short- and long-term memory. You need to remember short-term instructions for how to do projects, take tests, and follow directions. You need long-term memory for adding new information to your memory closet.

In English class you need to remember what the story was about and grammar rules. In History there are specific facts and people that have to be remembered. Math facts need to be stored and recalled so you can build upon the information at another time.

Most information has to step through short-term memory to get to the long-term memory part of the memory "closet." Here are a few ways to help you make the most of your memory.

3 Techniques to Help You Remember

1. SQ3R Method—Survey, Question, Read, Recite, Review

Surveying gives you an idea of what the book or chapter is about. Skim through for main ideas by looking at the headings, pictures, tables, and charts.

Questioning is the next step. Turn the headings into questions about the material.

◎ What are the names of the Great Lakes?

Read to find out the answers to the questions and underline important points.

Recite the information so you can hear it.

◎ Lake Huron, Lake Ontario, Lake Michigan, Lake Erie, Lake Superior.

Review. Look over and make sure you understand the material. Go over the review or study questions.

2. Organize information in groups.

Make **lists, charts, wheels and spokes,** and **"map"** information, according to what comes next. See the examples below.

United States Bodies of Water

Atlantic Ocean
Chesapeake Bay
St. Lawrence
Great Lakes (5)
Gulf of Mexico
Pacific Ocean

U.S. Explorers	
NAME	DISCOVERED
Ponce DeLeon	Florida
Columbus	America
LaSalle	Mississippi River
Balboa	Pacific Ocean

3. Use mnemonics

Take the first letter of key words to form a word or sentence that will give you clues about what you need to remember.

Example: **HOMES**—The great lakes of Huron, Ontario, Michigan, Erie, Superior.

Example: **Karen Poured Coffee On Fran's Good Shirt**—Kingdom, Phylum, Classification, Order, Family, Genus, Species (Science Classification)

There are a lot of good techniques and strategies for making the most of your memory. Check the library for books on good study skills or talk to your counselor for some help on what works best for you. Also check out the list of books at the end of this chapter.

ATTENTION

Paying attention means being able to concentrate on something for a length of time. As you get older (mature) and further along in school, it gets more important to work on something by yourself for a long time. This could mean listening to an instructor (teacher) explain something for 20 to 40 minutes. It could mean reading the whole chapter of your history book at one time.

Another description for paying attention is staying focused. To complete a job, you need the ability to stay focused. To do this, sometimes you have to tune out distractions. This is hard to do and takes a lot of practice and a conscientious effort. For example, imagine that someone is talking when your favorite TV show is on. You try very hard to listen to the show so you don't miss the action. Paying attention means you can "stay tuned" to the job you are supposed to be doing.

4 Ways to Help You with Attention

1. Find the best time to do your homework. Some students work best right after school and others immediately after supper. Find out which works best for you and work at that same time each day.

2. Practice keeping yourself "tuned into" the work you need to do. Set a goal of so much work to be finished in 10 minutes. Then work without distractions for that time. Use a watch with an alarm to keep track of the minutes. Examples:

- ◎ "I will learn 3 spelling words in 10 minutes."
- ◎ "By 7:10 I will have 3 math problems finished."
- ◎ "I will know 5 vocabulary words in 10 minutes."

3. In school, sit close to the teacher and blackboard. It is easier to pay attention if you are close to the action.

4. Your doctor may prescribe certain medicine to help you pay attention. These are stimulants and they help you to stay alert. They work something like the caffeine found in coffee.

Talk with your physician if you notice problems with the following:

- ◎ Being easily distracted
- ◎ Having trouble finishing assignments or chores
- ◎ Being disorganized and often losing things
- ◎ Talking at inappropriate times
- ◎ Inconsistency in school work. Some days you do a really good job on an assignment, and other days you can't seem to get anything right.

These problems may be signs that you would benefit from medication. If you are prescribed medication, remember that medication use should always be monitored by your doctor.

ORGANIZATION

Organization means the arrangement of things in a certain order. Being organized means having a place for everything and knowing where that place is. In school work, it means knowing what the work is, getting that work finished, and turning the work in when it is due. It can also mean keeping your work in an organized way or keeping your supplies organized.

Some people just seem to be born very organized. Others find it is a constant challenge to stay organized. A lot of people with spina bifida say they really have to work at organization; it doesn't come easy.

Students with spina bifida have a lot to keep track of. They must always be problem solving about getting around with a different kind of mobility—wheelchair, walker, or crutches. People without spina bifida have an internal alarm that tells them when to use the bathroom, but people with spina bifida even have to organize that!

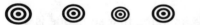

"The way I stay organized is to just keep things straight and try to know where everything is. I just do one thing at a time." - B.K.A.

Developing and practicing good organizational skills will be one of the best gifts you can give yourself. Being organized will make your memory much more efficient because you will know where things are. Being organized will make your life more comfortable and less stressed, especially when it is time to leave for school or work in the morning. Keeping things organized will help you to feel more "in control" and effective. You will be less likely to misplace assignments or to leave without materials or personal care supplies. Here are five tips that will help to develop some organization in your life.

5 Tips for Organizing Your School Life

1. Follow the same routine every day. If you do the same thing every day at the same time, you will develop a pattern. If you forget to do part of the job, it will feel funny and you will be reminded to think about what you may have forgotten. This is helpful in organizing your hygiene habits or developing study habits.

2. Keep your supplies for school together in a backpack. At night when you finish your homework, pack up your backpack with everything you will need for school so the only thing you have to do is pick it up in the morning.

3. Keep your school papers and homework in one place. Some students like to use 8-pocket folders. There is a pocket for each subject and you can keep your homework in the pocket also. When your teacher asks for the homework to be turned in, all your homework will be in one place, but each subject in a different pocket. This is especially useful if you have a duplicate set of books at home and another set at school. Your 8-pocket folder is what you will carry back and forth with all your assignments.

4. Write it down and check it off when complete. Use an assignment book, planner, or "To Do" list. All business executives have a planner and calendar. Take a lesson from them and use one for yourself. Write down your assignments, due dates for projects and homework, and test dates.

5. Anticipate. Get in the habit of thinking ahead or "rehearsing" what you will need for an activity. Hygiene supplies, specific clothes, medicine. Write down what you will need and check the list before you leave for school or activities.

WRITING

Writing is a skill that involves coordinating hand movements with input from the eye and mind. Writing combines thinking, memory, language, attention, and fine motor skills. All of these must go on at the same time. When you think about it, writing is a very complex activity.

Some students are able to negotiate with their teacher to adjust the amount of written work required and evaluate their knowledge another way. Some teachers will balance written work with other projects. If writing is difficult for you, talk with your teacher or tutor about other ways to evaluate what you have learned.

Although teachers may modify some writing requirements for you, other written assignments will probably remain an important part of your work. This is especially true in the upper levels of school. Taking notes, writing reports, and taking tests are traditional parts of school that exercise your ability to remember many different things, to organize ideas, and to communicate them to others. The next sections offer suggestions to help you deal with some typical writing difficulties.

3 Strategies to Use for Writing Compositions

1. **Brainstorm** your ideas down on paper before you begin so you can organize your thoughts.

2. **Write reports a little at a time.** Divide the report up and work on one section at a time.

3. **Negotiate with your teacher about answering essay questions on tests.** Here are some questions you might ask:
   - ◎ "Will you accept an outline for the answers instead of complete sentences?"
   - ◎ "Will you give me extra credit if my "brainstorming" paper has good points included?
   - ◎ "Can I have more time to take my test?"
   - ◎ "Can I take my test orally?"

6 Strategies for Taking Notes

1. **Pair up with another note taker** to compare, review, and fill in notes.

2. **Tape record the class** and refer to the tape when reviewing notes.

3. **Ask the teacher for a copy of the class outline** and then fill in important points.

4. Use the Cornell Notetaking System. You take traditional notes on the right side of the page, leaving space to go back and write your own notes and comments on the left side. See the example below.

	History
1st president	Gen. Washington
	my notes my notes my notes my notes
	my notes my notes my notes my notes
Important date	July 4, 1776
	my notes my notes my notes my notes
	my notes my notes my notes my notes
	my notes my notes my notes my notes

5. Use visuals, diagrams, and charts to help organize notes.

Laws That Affect Students with Disabilities

Section 504 Rehab. Act	IDEA Law	Title II ADA	Title III ADA
my notes my notes my notes my notes my notes my notes my notes notes my notes my notes	my notes my notes notes my notes my notes my notes my notes my notes	my notes my notes my notes my notes my notes my notes my notes my	my notes my notes my notes my notes my notes my notes my notes my notes
Enforced By:			
Office of Civil Rights	Office of Special Ed.	Civil Rights Dept. of Justice	Civil Rights Dept. of Justice

6. Develop your own shorthand system. Use your own abbreviations or symbols for words you use often. For example, use b/c for because; n'l for national.

3 Strategies for Better Writing Mechanics

1. Proofread your work at least two times. The first time check for the answer—to be sure you focused on the topic. The second proof should be for grammar, punctuation, and spelling. If you are writing a paper, have another person proofread once more before you make the final copy.

2. Use a typewriter or word processor. Most word processing programs have a spell check and some even have a grammar check. There are new programs that even speak the words as you write them. Learning to use a word processor or computer may be as difficult as writing at first, but if you practice, you will be able to produce very professional looking writing. Also, computer skills will be expected in the job market.

3. Use aids and gadgets for writing help.

◎ A hand-held electronic spell checker.

◎ An electronic memory reminder—a small gadget that lets you record 40 to 90 seconds of reminders. You can use this to record homework details; ideas for projects; things to do list.

◎ Computer programs for word processing and writing that make it easy to correct grammar, word usage, punctuation, and spelling.

Special Education Services

You may be receiving special education services through a federal law called IDEA (Individuals with Disabilities Education Act) and some other federal and state laws. The IDEA says you have the right to a free, appropriate education—an education that takes your special needs into account and is provided at no cost to your family. You also have the right to *related services* that are necessary to help you learn in school. These might include tutoring, resource room, special accommodations for writing, physical or occupational therapy, and even arrangements for catheterization.

These special education accommodations will be written into your IEP (Individualized Education Program). The law says the IEP should be reviewed and updated with new goals each year. You should be encouraged to participate in these IEP meetings, together with your teachers and parents. By the time you are 16, your IEP should include a Transition Plan. This is a plan for what you intend to do after high school and how you intend to achieve your goal. For instance, you might plan to attend a four-year college, community college, or vocational school or to get a job. How you will explore these possibilities at school should be written in your Transition Plan.

If you are approaching college, you can also apply for special testing circumstances for the ACT's or SAT's. This may include extended testing time or having the test read to you. Talk with your counselor, tutor, or the SAT Services for Students with Disabilities, the College Board, P.O. Box 6226, Princeton, New Jersey 08541-6226.

Wrap Up

Research has proven that students with spina bifida have definite differences in their bodies that affect learning. These may be due to actual differences in nervous system structure, surgeries, or medication. Because of these differences, some students with spina bifida have more difficulty in school than usual. You will need to be aware of both your special strengths and difficulties in learning. You will need to communicate with your teacher about the best way you learn. This will help you receive the good and challenging education you need to achieve your personal best. Practice the strategies in this chapter, think positive, and build on your strengths!

Educational Resources

HEATH Resource Center
One Dupont Circle
Washington, DC 20036
1-800-54-HEATH

Information for postsecondary (after high school) education for individuals with disabilities. Excellent resource for information on accommodations for persons with learning differences, special schools, programs, financial aid, etc.

NICHCY
National Information Center for Children & Youth with Disabilities
P.O. Box 1492
Washington, DC 20013-1492
1-800-695-0285

Collects and shares information and ideas that are helpful to children and youth with disabilities.

Parent Training & Information Centers
Federation for Children with Special Needs
312 Stuart Street
Boston, MA 02116
617-482-2915

Provides technical assistance & information on special accommodations and regional centers.

SAT Services for Students with Disabilities
P.O. Box 6226
Princeton, NJ 08541-6226
1-609-771-7137

Recording for the Blind & Dyslexic
20 Roszel Road
Princeton, New Jersey 08540
609-452-0606
1-800-221-4792

Nonprofit service organization that provides recorded textbooks, tape players, and other educational resources to individuals who cannot read standard print because of visual, physical, or perceptual disability.

Spina Bifida Association of America
4590 MacArthur Blvd.
Suite 250
Washington, DC 20007-4226
202-944-3285
1-800-621-3141

Association of persons with spina bifida, parents, and professionals. Provides support, information and referral to local chapters. Holds annual medical and educational national conferences and offers publications.

U.S. Dept. of Education
Office of Civil Rights
Washington, DC 20202

Information on laws affecting education.

Books for the Educational Experience

How to Choose a College: Guide for the Student with a Disability. Heath Resource Center, One Dupont Circle, Suite 800, Washington, DC 20036-1193 (free).

Keeping A Head In School: A Student's Book about Learning Abilities and Learning Disorders, by Dr. Mel Levine. Educators Publishing Services, 1990.

Negotiating the Special Education Maze: A Guide for Parents and Teachers, by Winifred Anderson, Stephen Chitwood, and Deidre Hayden. Woodbine House, 1997.

Putting on the Brakes, by Patricia O. Quinn. Magination Press, 1991.

The School Survival Guide for Kids with L.D. (Learning Differences): Ways to Make Learning Easier and More Fun, by Rhoda Cummings and Gary Fisher. Free Spirit Publishing Co., 1991. (Also available as an audio cassette.)

Succeeding Against the Odds: Strategies and Insights from the Learning Disabled, by Sally L. Smith. G.P. PutnamP's Sons, 1991.

The Survival Guide for Teenagers with L.D. (Learning Differences), by Rhoda Cummings and Gary Fisher. Free Spirit Publishing Co., 1993. (Also available as an audio cassette.)

Teaching the Student with Spina Bifida, by Fern L. Rowley, Kelly & Donald H. Reigel, M.D. Paul Brookes Publishing, 1993.

11

Payday

(Career Planning)

Linda Custis-Allen, M.S., OTR/L

Hi Ho, Hi Ho, it's off to work we go. . . .

Are you prepared for the world of work? If not, read this chapter for ideas. It covers many of the things you can do to get ready:

◎ Develop Skills and Gain Experiences
◎ Know Your Rights
◎ Take Advantage of Vocational Training or Advanced Education
◎ Learn about Your Job Interests

Getting Ready

Preparation for a career doesn't happen overnight. It doesn't happen because you are 18 years old or 21 years old. It doesn't happen just because you graduated from high school. If you think about it, preparation for work began when you were born. Skills you learned as a baby (learning to talk, taking turns) and in elementary school (learning to read and write, finishing work on time) are important for career preparation.

Career preparation means using your time and energy *now* to develop skills and gain experiences that will help you find a job *later.* Your skills and experiences will help an employer decide whether to hire you.

Develop Skills and Gain Experiences

CHOOSE ACTIVITIES WISELY

The activities that you choose now can help you become active and ready for work. Here are some activities you might try that will help you develop skills and gain experiences.

- Volunteer.
- Learn to play a musical instrument.
- Attend summer camp.
- Join the church choir.
- Participate with a school athletic team.
- Join a club at school or in your community.
- Participate in the school science fair.
- Work at a part-time job.
- Learn computer keyboard skills.

LEARN SKILLS

There are certain skills that everyone needs in order to be prepared for work. Acquiring some of these skills may take more effort for young people with spina bifida. If you start working on them while you are still in school, however, you should be prepared by the time you are ready to look for a job.

Self-Care Skills

Employers hire people who are neat, independent, and well groomed. If you need ideas about dressing, grooming, or transfers, try the suggestions in Chapter 2.

Bowel and Bladder Skills

When working with others, you will feel more confident if you don't have to worry about wetness or odor. If you have trouble with continence, try the ideas in Chapters 4 and 5.

Decision-Making Skills

Success on the job depends on making good decisions. If you need practice making decisions, begin with simple decisions, such as:

◎ What to wear to school?

◎ What to eat for lunch?

◎ What time to get up in the morning?

◎ What clubs or activities to join?

Work up to more difficult decisions:

◎ What classes/courses to take at school?

◎ When to make a dentist appointment or doctor appointment?

◎ What clothes to buy?

Eventually, you will be ready for adult decisions:

◎ What kind of job?

◎ Where to live?

◎ How to spend/save money?

◎ Whether to get married?

◎ Whether to have children?

If your parents are making decisions for you that you feel you can make, now is the time to talk with them. Tell them that you would like to begin making some of these decisions. Let them know how much you appreciate them and that you hope they will remain available for advice.

Skills for Getting Around

Most people work some place other than their home. This means it's important to be able to travel independently to and from work. You might walk to work, drive a car, or take public transportation.

If you've never used the bus or subway to get yourself to the mall for shopping or to a movie with a friend, try it. See if public transportation can work for you.

Call for information about public transportation. Look in the Yellow Pages of the phone book under "Transportation" and/or "Bus Lines." Make calls to check on the cost of taxi cabs in your area.

Maybe your city does not have bus service or you cannot get to the bus stop. If so, find out what kind of transportation your city has for people who have physical disabilities. Some cities have buses equipped with wheelchair lifts. Your city may also have specialized buses or vans that go door to door. Ask a friend, your doctor, a nurse, or a therapist about special transportation.

Learning to drive may be another option for you. There are hand controls that attach to the steering wheel for people who cannot operate foot pedals. Ask around in your community to find out where you can go to learn how to drive, or try the ideas in Chapter 6. Think about how you would manage the expense of driving a car. Gasoline, insurance, and repairs cost money.

Skills for Managing Money

People who make money must learn how to manage it. Here are some ideas for getting the practice you need.

Ask for an allowance to spend on clothes, activities, and supplies. It is a good idea to save some, too.

Go to the bank and open a savings and checking account. When you open your bank account, ask your parents or the banker to teach you how to write a check, about interest on savings, and how to use a credit card, debit card, and ATM (automatic teller machine) card.

Ask for jobs around the house and neighborhood. Maybe you can baby-sit, do laundry, wash dishes, or help clean. The possibilities are endless.

Learn how to manage your money to cover your expenses and save for your future. Ask that instruction about budgeting be included in your IEP (Individualized Education Program), Transition to Work Plan, or Section 504 Plan. If you are no longer in high school, ask for help at your bank. Call and make an appointment with a manager. Tell them that you need help managing your money.

Learn about paying taxes. The public library and post office have all the forms necessary for paying taxes. Ask a parent, older friend, or sibling to help you fill out your federal and state returns.

Work Related Skills

Employers hire people who do their best and have good work habits. They look for people who are punctual, friendly, ambitious, and dependable. To practice these good work habits:

◎ Complete homework assignments on time. Be on time to meetings, appointments, lessons.
◎ Become a volunteer to get experience working with others.
◎ Get a part-time job.
◎ Be well-groomed, clean, and neatly dressed. Employers do not want to hire people who look sloppy and disorganized.
◎ Do your best on homework and jobs around the house.
◎ Pay attention to good manners—say "please" and "thank you." Remember that some employers may consider chewing gum bad manners.

You can be successful at work. Develop a positive work attitude!

Know Your Rights

Because our society values work, our government has passed laws to help people with disabilities become educated and find work. These laws make sure that you have:

1. Equal access to public education, services (libraries, museums, courts of law), transportation, and jobs.

2. An Individualized Education Program (IEP) or a 504 Plan to establish needs, services, and educational goals during your public school education.

3. A Transition to Work Plan included in your IEP or Section 504 Plan by age 16. This is a plan that identifies what you need to make the transition from school to work.

TIPS ON KNOWING YOUR RIGHTS

If you are in junior or senior high school, you should have a written IEP or Section 504 Plan. These plans can help identify your needs and plan for your future. For example, these plans can include strategies to help you learn to drive a car with hand controls, use public transportation, explore job opportunities, make plans for college, and improve banking skills. *All* students with spina bifida can benefit from an IEP or Section 504 Plan. By the time you are 16 years old, your IEP or Section 504 Plan should address transition to work. The Transition to Work Plan could include:

◎ Vocational assessment (testing) to predict the kind of job where you will be successful.
◎ Vocational training for a specific job.
◎ Instructional support such as tutoring or help with math or reading.

◎ Community experiences, which might include a volunteer or part-time job.

◎ On-the-job training at your work site.

◎ Planning for college.

◎ Planning for independent living.

You should attend and participate in your IEP, Section 504, and/or Transition to Work Plan meetings. Tell your school officials at this meeting about your needs and goals. For example, one of your long-term goals might be to have a full-time job by the time you graduate from high school. Your Transition to Work Plan might list these short-term goals to help meet your long-term goal.

◎ Student will have a vocational assessment to determine interests and strengths.

◎ Student will spend two hours a day working at school or in the community.

◎ Student will successfully manage his own transportation needs.

What if you have worked with your school and are not satisfied that a reasonable effort has been made to address your transition needs? If so, you may want to find an advocate or a lawyer to help you. To get help, look in the White Pages of your phone book and call Legal Aid Society, or look in the Yellow Pages and call Lawyer Referral and Information Services. Your spina bifida team may be able to refer you to other helpful agencies in your community.

TIPS ON EMPLOYMENT RIGHTS

The ADA (Americans with Disabilities Act) protects your rights to equal opportunity for jobs and services. It does so by prohibiting many different kinds of discrimination against people with disabilities. Where employment is concerned, the law says that:

1. An employer is not allowed to ask you about your disability during an interview or make you take a medical exam. (You do not need to include information about your disability on your resume or job applications.)

2. An employer may ask if you can perform specific job functions/activities. For example, could you deliver pizzas? Clear tables? Run a cash register?

3. An employer must make reasonable accommodations (changes) for your disability. For example, you might need to sit instead of stand to operate the cash register.

4. You will want to share your needs with your employer so that reasonable accommodations can be made. For example, you might need an accessible bathroom.

If you think you have been discriminated against, you can obtain a lawyer to help you. To get help, look in the White Pages of your phone book and call Legal Aid Society, or look in the Yellow Pages and call Lawyer Referral and Information Services. You can also file a complaint with the nearest office of the U.S. Equal Employment Opportunity Commission (EEOC). This office is usually listed in the white pages under U.S. Government. For further information about what the ADA says about employment, call the EEOC at 1-800-669-EEOC.

Take Advantage of Vocational Training or Advanced Education

The more education you have, the more choices you have for work and career. Many people find that a high school education is not enough. You may want to consider an educational program after high school to prepare you for work and career:

- ◎ Vocational education (hands-on training in job skills such as word processing, hair dressing, car repair)
- ◎ Junior or community college
- ◎ Technical education (training programs lasting several months to several years leading to specialized skills such as drafting, dental assisting, or commercial photography)
- ◎ College or university

Students with disabilities are eligible for accommodations at most colleges, universities, and training programs. This is because Section 504 prohibits schools that receive any federal funding from discriminating against people with disabilities. Helpful accommodations might include a special parking permit, a tape recorder for class notes, or extra time for taking tests and completing assignments. You can find out about accommodations and accessibility by:

◎ calling the school or program you are considering

◎ asking your guidance counselor

◎ looking at resources in your public library, such as *Colleges with Programs for Students with Learning Disabilities* (published by Peterson's Guides); or *Survival Guide for College Students with ADD or LD,* by Kathleen G. Nadeau.

"I want to do something in the clerical field in business. I went through three years of college to get an Associate's degree in business studies." - L.J.

If you decide to continue your education after high school, you'll have to decide whether to live at home or on campus. The advantages and disadvantages of each choice are basically the same for you as for anyone making this decision. For example, if you live at home, costs will be less. On the other hand, living on campus gives you the experience of being on your own.

Learn about Your Job Interests

Maybe you have known what you want to be when you "grow up" since you were a child. Maybe you feel as if you can't be anything else except an artist, a doctor, a teacher. . . . Most students, however, haven't chosen a definite career path by high school graduation. If you're in this group, you may wonder how to zero in on a good career for you. You can begin by looking at your own interests.

◎ Think about what kind of work you would feel comfortable and successful doing.

◎ Think about what is interesting to you.

◎ Think about what you are good at.

◎ Think about your personality. (Are you energetic? Outgoing? Do you like to work with others or work alone?)

◎ Think about your hobbies. How do you spend your free time?

◎ If you have had vocational testing, think about whether the results of the testing truly reflect your interests and abilities.

If you aren't sure what kind of job would fulfill your interests, try looking at things the other way around. Look at different jobs and think about whether they would interest you.

◎ When you are out, watch people working; ask questions about jobs.
◎ Talk to friends and people in your family about the work they do.
◎ Look at the "Help Wanted" ads in the newspaper.
◎ Talk to your counselor at school about jobs.

Get a Volunteer or Part-Time Job

Getting a volunteer or part-time job is a good way to explore career options and learn important job skills.

A volunteer is someone who does a job, but does not get paid money for the work. Many agencies need volunteers. Schools, zoos, retirement homes, hospitals, museums, political campaign offices, and public television stations are just a few examples. Many have organized volunteer programs and are looking for someone just like you. A volunteer job will help you gain experience for a later job. A volunteer job can:

◎ help you explore an area of interest for a possible career choice;
◎ help you get started in a career where jobs are scarce;
◎ look good on your resume;
◎ give you a feeling that you are making the world a better place;
◎ give you experience working with others;
◎ give you a chance to practice work skills.

A part-time job is a job that requires only a few hours each week (usually less than 30). Some people work part-time so they can also go to school. Some people work part-time, not full-time, so that their Social Security Income or medical coverage is not lost. A part-time job can help prepare you for a full-time job.

Getting a part-time or volunteer job takes thought and planning:

1. Think about how much spare time you have for work or volunteer activity.

2. Think about how you would get to and from a job or volunteer activity.

3. Prepare a resume. (See the next section.)

4. Many young people get part-time or volunteer jobs at a business where a relative or friend works. Ask your family or friends about this possibility.

5. Look in the newspaper for jobs.

6. Ask your counselor at school about volunteer or part-time jobs.

7. Identify a business that might give you a volunteer or part-time job. Call and ask for an interview or to complete an application.

8. Take your resume with you. You will look prepared and organized.

9. The first try at a volunteer or part-time job doesn't always work out. Sometimes the hours are wrong, or transportation doesn't work out. Or maybe it's a job that you just don't like. These things happen, so just keep trying.

There are lots of opportunities; don't limit yourself. Every job is a learning experience that will help you gain important skills.

How to Prepare a Resume

A resume is an advertisement about you. It tells a person who might hire you for a job all about you. It stresses your good points and skills. Here (on the next page) is a sample you could copy.

Make sure your resume is typed neatly with correct spelling and information. Take it with you to a job interview, to leave with the interviewer. Also take it with you to complete an application. (You can copy correct information from your resume onto the application or include it with your application.)

"It was on my first job. I dropped a tub of dishes on the floor in front of customers. I handled it by kind of laughing at it. I did, however, apologize to my boss later for breaking the dishes."—KS

Get Help with Career Planning

If you have read this chapter, tried the ideas, and still need help with career planning, here are some agencies and organizations that might help you.

Jane A. Smith
555 Ash Lane
Cincinnati, Ohio 55555
Telephone: (555) 555-5555

Personal:
Date of Birth - 4/18/78
Place of Birth - Indianapolis, Indiana
Marital Status - Single
Height - 5'2"   Weight - 125 lbs.
Health - Excellent
Social Security Number - 555-55-5555
[Most of this personal information is optional.]

Education:
Public High School, Cincinnati, Ohio
Currently in senior year

Extracurricular Activities:
Spanish Club, Senior Choir, guitar lessons, student newspaper reporter

Skills:
Experience in WordPerfect 6.0
Type 30 words per minute

Experience:
Volunteer at: Hospital Medical Center
                       555 Fifth Avenue
                       Cincinnati, Ohio
                       June 1993 to present

Baby-sitting 1992 to present

References:
Mrs. Linda Williams, Junior Volunteer Coordinator
Hospital Medical Center—(555) 555-5555

Mrs. Donna Jones, Baby-sitting employer
(555) 555-5555

Mrs. Rebecca Allen, Baby-sitting employer
(555) 555-5555

Agencies That Help

Vocational Rehabilitation

is a nationwide program for helping people with disabilities prepare for and find work. If you are old enough to work, this agency can help you. Services include evaluation, counseling, obtaining aids and devices, and job placement. Look for the phone number under your state name, followed by Division, Department, or Bureau of Rehabilitation Services or Vocational Rehabilitation Services.

Goodwill Industries

provides job training to men and women with disabilities who are at least 18 years old. Goodwill Industries offers a range of services, including work evaluation, occupational skills training, supportive employment, and job placement. Jobs may be at a Goodwill Agency or in the community. There are 179 locations in North America. You can find the location near you by looking in the phone book under Goodwill Industries, or you can write or call the national office at:

> Goodwill Industries
> 9200 Wisconsin Avenue
> Bethesda, MD 20814-3896
> Phone: 301-530-6500
> TTY: 301-530-9759
> Fax: 301-530-1516

Jewish Vocational Services provides a broad range of vocational services to help people with disabilities obtain employment and fit into the community. Services provided include on-site training, job coaching, job placement, work adjustment training, etc. Jewish Vocational Services provides services to the total community. For a location near you, look in the white pages of your phone book, or write or call:

International Association of Jewish Vocational Services
1845 Walnut Street, Suite 608
Philadelphia, PA 19103
Phone: 215-854-0233

United Cerebral Palsy Associations has more than 150 centers nationwide. They provide therapeutic, educational, and support programs to people of all ages who have disabilities. The goal of UCPA is to encourage and enable people with disabilities to participate fully in life and society. The range of services is different from center to center. Services at some centers might include: social skills training, supported employment, computer skills training, training in using attendant care, independent living skills, and others. (Supported employment means finding out what kind of job a person wants, and providing assistance such as job coaching until the employee can independently perform the position.)

To find out about services at a center near you, look in the phone book under United Cerebral Palsy Association, or you can write or call the National Association at:

United Cerebral Palsy Associations
1660 L Street, N.W., Suite 700
Washington, DC 20036-5602
Phone: 1-800-872-5827

The **National Council on Independent Living** is a network of 400 agencies. These agencies provide services to people of all ages who have disabilities. Services related to preparation for work include:

◎ housing information
◎ independent living skills training
◎ community service information and referral
◎ attendant care assistance
◎ peer support

For the location of an agency near you, write or call:

The National Council on Independent Living
2111 Wilson Blvd.
Suite 405
Arlington, Virginia 22201
Phone: 703-525-3406
TTY: 703-525-3407
Fax: 703-525-3409

ORGANIZATIONS THAT HELP

You might get ideas for preparing for work from local or national support organizations:

- ◎ Your church or religious group
- ◎ Big Brothers or Big Sisters
- ◎ Boy Scouts and Girl Scouts or 4-H Club
- ◎ The Spina Bifida Association

The Spina Bifida Association of America (SBAA) is a network of local groups (chapters) across the country. These chapters provide support and information to people with spina bifida and their families. The Adult Network provides opportunities for adults with spina bifida to learn about:

- ◎ health;
- ◎ independent living;
- ◎ career development; and
- ◎ participation in society.

To find a local chapter or to learn about the Adult Network contact:

The Spina Bifida Association of America
4590 MacArthur Boulevard, N.W.
Suite 250
Washington, DC 20007-4226
Phone: 202-944-3285; 1-800-621-3141
Fax: 202-944-3295

You can be successful at work: Develop a positive attitude!

Additional Information

For free or low cost federal publications on topics such as:

- ◎ Employment,
- ◎ Federal Help for Individuals with Disabilities,
- ◎ The ADA: Questions and Answers,

call the Federal Information Center at 1-800-688-9889 and request a Consumer Information Catalog from Pueblo. Or you can write to the address below and request a catalog to find and order the publications you want.

Consumer Information Center
P.O. Box 100
Pueblo, CO 81002

Are You Ready for Work?

So, are you ready for work? Answer these questions to find out.

	True	False
1. I believe that I am capable of work, and I expect to have a job some day.		
2. I am independent with dressing, hygiene, and transfers.		
3. I manage my bowel and bladder and stay clean and dry.		
4. I can use public transportation or drive a car.		
5. I know how to save money and use money to pay for things.		
6. I spend time thinking about the kind of work I want to do.		
TOTAL		

If you answered true to all of these statements, you are doing great. Keep it up. You are on the road to work. If you answered false to any statement, you'll need to make a change. Decide to learn the skills you need to get ready for work! Talk to your parents, health care professionals, and/or your IEP team for help. *You* can be successful at work!

PART FOUR

Healthy

Practices

12

Healthy Practices

Marlene Lutkenhoff, R.N., M.S.N.

The body is an amazing thing. To keep running smoothly, though, it needs a certain amount of upkeep from you—the owner. It is important to take care of your body so that it can do its job to keep you healthy. This chapter covers some of the many habits you can develop and practice to take care of your emotional and physical health. It discusses:

- ◎ Coping with emotions;
- ◎ Nutrition and weight control;
- ◎ Alcohol and drugs;
- ◎ Safety; and
- ◎ Routine medical care.

Dealing with Feelings

Everyone has feelings. Feelings can change from day to day. It's important to know that feelings of anger, sadness, frustration, fear, happiness, kindness, and loneliness are all O.K. feelings. All teenagers and adults feel sad sometimes and happy at other times. In other words, having periods of ups and downs is a part of living. Learning how to handle these ups and downs in a healthy way is part of growing up.

Sometimes you may have strong feelings related to having spina bifida. You may not know how to handle your feelings or who can help you deal with them. This section points out some good ways and bad ways of handling your feelings.

ANGER

It's easy to get angry if someone makes unkind or untrue remarks about your disability. Some young people with spina bifida react by saying something equally unkind or by doing something to get revenge. Some people fight and punch when they get angry. Usually, none of these responses help. They don't make you feel any better about what happened.

A better response is to walk away from someone who is making you angry. This puts you in control instead of out of control. Later, when you feel calm, you can go back to the person who made you angry and *let him know how it made you feel.* You could say something like "when you laughed at me because I had trouble opening the door, it made me sad. It would have been nicer if you had asked if you could help me. Some things are hard for me and I would have appreciated your help." When you respond this way, you teach others something of value.

SADNESS

Having a physical disability means learning how to live with limitations. There are many things you may think you can never do, like playing baseball, or dancing, or just being able to get up and go without your wheelchair and braces. At times, you may feel sad about what you cannot do. You may want to be alone and sometimes cry.

Short periods of sadness are normal for all people. Most of the time, sad feelings come and go. When you feel sad, think about something you can do that makes you feel good or happy. Maybe for you that means visiting a friend or shopping or going to a movie. Another helpful thing to do is to talk to someone about your feelings, someone who can help you by listening to you and then reminding you about your good qualities, like how kind you are or how good you are at swimming. When you start thinking about good things, it's harder to feel sad and depressed.

It's only when you feel sad most or all of the time that it becomes a problem. If this happens, you might feel tired all the time, yet might have trouble sleeping. When sadness leads to depression, you often lose interest in all activities and find yourself alone more and more. If you are depressed, you may become negative, grouchy, aggressive, and uncooperative. You may become moody and feel anxious and irritable. Sleeping and eating habits often are affected. Sometimes you may not feel good about life in general.

When you're really depressed, there may not be anything you can do by yourself to make things better. Seeing a professional counselor or taking medicines may be necessary for a period of time. Usually the best way to find a counselor is to ask your doctor for a referral. You can also look under "Mental Health Services" in the Yellow Pages to find agencies that provide counseling.

> "I think that my biggest achievement in life is getting as far as I have without feeling sorry for myself. I think that even though I am disabled, not thinking that I am disabled has helped me."—B.S.

It's a fact, life isn't fair, but we all need to learn to live with that fact.

LONELINESS

Having a chronic disability can make you feel isolated (separate) from others around you. It's true that no one really knows what living with spina bifida is like but you. At times you may feel like an outsider. It is important, though, not to isolate yourself from others.

People with spina bifida meet other people and potential friends the same way other people do. Joining groups that do activities you enjoy is a good way to keep from feeling lonely. You may have to make yourself go to that first meeting or two, but eventually, as you get to know the others, you will find yourself looking forward to going. Joining one group can lead to increased opportunities for telephone conversations and activities outside the group with people you become friends with. Sometimes it helps to talk to others who know what it's like to have spina bifida. The National Spina Bifida Association can probably put you in touch with other young people.

FRUSTRATION/RESENTMENT

Not being able to do everything your friends can do can lead to frustration and resentment. This can be easier said than done, but try not to think about things you can't do. Instead, concentrate on things you can do. In most instances, you will find that you can do about anything you set your mind to.

There is a host of adaptive equipment available to help you with your personal or recreational needs. The wheelchair itself has become highly streamlined and efficient, making it possible for you to play competitive sports, such as basketball, baseball, and road racing, to name a few. A sit ski or mono-ski is available for those who cannot use their lower legs, yet want to ski. Today, many parks are accessible and some have trails that accommodate people in wheelchairs. Even young children are finding that they can enjoy biking with their friends with the use of hand-propelled bicycles.

If you just can't figure out a way to do something with friends, talk to them about your frustrations. Be tactful so you don't sound like you resent them for not having a disability. Maybe your friends will be willing to adapt their activities to you. It doesn't help to just stew about something when your friends might be able to help you with it.

Eating Wisely

Your body needs carbohydrates, proteins, fats, vitamins, minerals, and water every day. If you choose a variety of foods from the various food groups, you will be giving your body what it needs.

Milk Group	Fruit & Vegetable	Meat Group	Grain Group
milk	beans	meats	bread
butter	tomatoes	fish	noodles
cheese	corn	eggs	rice
ice cream	spinach	nuts	crackers
yogurt	apples	dried beans	cereal
	grapes	peas	
	berries		

How much food you need every day depends on your size, age, weight, sex, body chemistry, and activity. Everything you eat contains calories. Some foods produce more calories than others. (See "Counting Calories," below.) You may not need as many calories as your friends. For one reason, you may be shorter than your friends, so your smaller size limits the amount of calories you need. For another reason, your activity may be limited because of your physical disability. You may not be able to do some activities that would help you burn calories, like jogging, riding a bike, or maybe even walking.

If you take in more calories than your body needs, you will gain weight. Being overweight is hard on your body. Your heart must work harder and your muscles will tire faster. Most people have difficulty losing weight. People with spina bifida who are in wheelchairs can have an extremely hard time losing weight because of limited activity. That is why it is so much better to eat just the right amount of food to keep your weight within a desired range. Your doctor can tell you what is a good weight for you and about how many calories you need a day to maintain that weight.

COUNTING CALORIES

Some foods have lots of calories, particularly foods that contain lots of fat, starch, and sugar. Foods high in calories should be eaten occasionally or not at all if you are trying to lose weight.

The chart below gives you an idea of the calorie count of a few foods.

FOOD	CALORIES
1 cup 2% low fat milk	121
chocolate milk shake	320
12 ounce Coke	151
fast food hamburger	500
small serving french fries	220
1 slice pizza	185
15 potato chips	172
1 cup unbuttered popcorn	25
orange	63
apple	80
½ baked chicken breast	142
1 cup boiled broccoli	50

Let's say you went out to lunch and had:

Fast food hamburger	500
Fries (small)	+ 220
Coke	+ 151
	871

You would have consumed around 800 to 900 calories at *one* meal. That's a lot of calories, especially if you need less than 1500 for the entire day. In that case, you only have 600 calories left to divide among breakfast, dinner, and snacks.

If you primarily use your wheelchair to get around, chances are you need less than 1500 calories to maintain your current weight. If you want to lose weight, you need less.

If you walk pretty much all of the day and are fairly active, you may be able to handle 2000 calories a day without gaining weight.

Another way to help you lose weight, besides eating less, is doing more. Everything you do burns calories. If you want to lose weight, you need to find activities you can do that will help you use up calories. The harder you work at the activity, the more calories you will burn.

The chart below gives you an idea of the calories burned per hour for certain activities.

Activity	Calories Burned Per Hour
Watching TV	50-100
Walking	160-310
Swimming	300-700
Reading	22
Making your bed	169
Bicycling	300-700

Remember, too many calories + too little exercise = too much weight.

Before attempting to lose weight, talk to your family physician and/or nutritionist. Dieting may affect your bowel program. A nutritionist will be able to suggest high fiber foods low in calories.

Handling Alcohol and Drugs

Drinking alcohol, smoking, or using drugs causes problems for many people, including people with spina bifida. The fact is, these drugs harm all of us. The best way to prevent drug abuse is to be aware of their harmful effects and make wise decisions.

ALCOHOL

Alcohol is a depressant, which means it slows down the body's functions. Someone under the influence of alcohol has trouble thinking and a slower reaction time. That is why so many people who drink and drive have accidents. Alcohol can also lead to stomach ulcers and kidney disease. Alcoholism (addiction to alcohol) is a disease that in many cases leads to death.

At the proper age, and at the proper time, alcohol in moderation is O.K. Although it is O.K. for adults to have an alcoholic beverage from time to time, it should never be used to help someone forget about their troubles. When the alcohol wears off, the problems are still there. Many people with spina bifida take a medication called Ditropan™. Alcohol can increase the side effects of drowsiness, blurred vision, and dizziness that some people experience when taking this medication.

TOBACCO

Smoking tobacco is bad for your body. It can lead to diseases of the heart and blood vessels. It produces harmful effects on the lungs. Have you ever heard a smoker cough that dry, hacking cough? Pretty horrible sounding, isn't it?

For people with spina bifida, smoking may be even more harmful. Many people with spina bifida develop scoliosis. Scoliosis and other backbone problems reduce lung capacity and make breathing more difficult. Long-term smoking and reduced lung capacity spell double trouble.

DRUGS

Experimenting with drugs such as marijuana, uppers, downers, and inhalants is dangerous. The problem with most of these types of drugs is that people become addicted to them. Overdoses are common and often result in death.

Sometimes your friends may try to tell you that taking a certain drug such as an upper will make you feel better. Friends can be very convincing and it's hard to say no when the people you are with are all participating. Stop and think about what you believe in and what you think is right. Have the courage to stick with your beliefs.

Safety

Fire safety is a big issue for people with physical disabilities. You need to be able to get out of your house quickly in case of a fire. If you use a wheelchair, that might mean putting ramps outside doors. Having more than one way out is also important. Plan and practice several escape routes. Your family or the fire department can help you with planning. Smoke detectors and fire extinguishers are good things to have in your home. Know how to call the fire department, police, and emergency medical people in your area.

Taking automotive safety seriously is another thing that can help you stay alive and well. Always wear a seat belt when riding in a car. If you drive, keep your car in good condition by having it serviced regularly. You may also want to invest in a cellular phone so you can call for help in an emergency.

Routine Medical Care

If you see a variety of specialists for different medical needs, it may be tempting to let routine medical care slide. This is a mistake. If you take the time for routine medical and dental checkups and to monitor your own health, many problems can be detected and treated before they become serious.

You should see your family physician twice a year for a physical exam. He or she will examine you and ask you questions to make sure your body is working as it should. You should also see a dentist once a year for a dental exam, cleaning of teeth, and X-rays. (And, of course, you should brush and floss daily to keep your gums and teeth in good shape between visits.)

For Women Only. If you are over the age of 18, you should have a gynecological (pelvic) exam and a Pap test once a year. (See Chapter 9 for more information.) Whatever your age, you should also examine your breasts about once a month to look for possible lumps. This exam is easy to do, but should be done in a certain way. Ask a doctor or nurse to show you the first time.

For Men Only. About once a month, males should examine their testicles (balls) to look for possible lumps. A good time is after a shower or bath. Gently roll each testicle between thumb and fingers of both hands for several minutes. If you know the feel and shape of your testicles, you will be able to notice lumps or swelling immediately and be able to check with your physician.

Your Special Medical Needs

As you already know, people with spina bifida often have special medical needs. Right now, your parents may take the responsibility for making sure these needs are monitored and treated. But your parents will not always be around to help you. And there may not always be a clinic where you can go to get help. This makes it important that you begin to understand all about your body, and to learn how to make medical appointments and know when and how to get help. Remember that headaches may mean you are under a lot of stress or may be the first sign of a shunt problem. A fever may signify a simple cold or a nasty urinary infection. A change in the way your feet or legs look or function may mean there is a problem inside the spinal cord. You need to visit the doctor regularly and whenever you don't feel right.

Taking over your medical care will take time and patience. You will need to ensure that you see specialists and your primary physician on a regular basis. As you get older, you probably won't need to see the specialists as often. The primary physician will be able to monitor a lot of your care. He or she will refer you to a specialist if there is a need. Obviously, if you don't have a primary physician, it's important to find one.

Since you have spina bifida, it is important to find someone who is knowledgeable about your disability. The best way to find a good doctor is to ask others who they go to and whether they are satisfied. You might ask your spina bifida team for a referral.

When you visit your doctor, don't be afraid to ask questions. If you don't understand something, ask your doctor to explain it another way. If your parents go along with you, the doctor should speak to you, not your parents. *You* should answer the doctor's questions. A good doctor is someone you can trust and someone who listens to you. If you are not happy with your doctor, by all means, find another one. You may have to check with your insurance before switching, however.

If your parents are making your medical appointments and you feel ready to take control, tell them. Most likely, they will be thrilled with your desire to be more independent. Ask them to explain what type of insurance you have and how to file important papers. Insurance forms are complicated for everybody. You might want to begin by first filling the papers out yourself and having your parents go over them. Your parents will likely be happy to continue helping you until you feel confident to take over.

Turn page for another checklist ▷ ▷ ▷

Health-Care Checklist

Directions: Read the statements and see how many are true for you.

	True	False
1. I call to schedule medical/dental appointments on a regular basis.		
2. I have found a physician to call who is knowledgeable about my disability and understands my needs.		
3. I understand and am able to describe my health care needs.		
4. I ask questions of health care professionals.		
5. I am able to call the doctor or pharmacist to refill prescriptions when needed and understand what medications are for.		
6. I carry medical insurance information with me.		
TOTAL		

These statements describe ways you can take an active role in caring for your medical needs. Any "false" responses will show you which areas you need to work on.

13

Basic Training

(Fitness, Exercise, and Sports)

Catherine Lowe, M.S., P.T.

Exercise is a part of good health for everyone. Flexibility, aerobic, and weight training exercises strengthen the heart and lungs and improve muscle strength and endurance. If you have spina bifida, you have even more reasons to exercise. To use crutches, a walker, or wheelchair and still keep up, you need more strength and endurance than your friends without spina bifida. When you have spina bifida, you are also more likely to gain weight. If you become heavier, you may develop pressure sores and lose your ability to walk. For these reasons, exercise is important to help you keep up, keep fit, and keep going!

A good exercise program consists of three parts:

1. warm up,
2. exercise, and
3. cool down.

The purpose of warming up is to increase muscle temperature and prepare the muscles for aerobic or weight training. Just like a car in the winter, your

"Wheeling a mile is the healthiest thing I do for myself."—K.C.

muscles need time to warm up to run smoothly. Warm up exercises can include shoulder rolls, arm circles, or slow wheelchair laps. Walking or riding a stationary bike can prepare muscles for leg exercises. When you start to sweat, you have warmed up enough. Following exercise, a five- to ten-minute cool down period can include stretches and activity such as walking or slow wheelchair laps.

So . . . warm up first . . . then exercise . . . then cool your body down.

Flexibility Training

Flexibility training, or stretching, is an important part of warm up and cool down. It is especially important for people with spina bifida, who are more likely to develop contractures due to muscle weakness, paralysis, and imbalance. A contracture is a shortened or tight muscle that limits movement around a particular joint. Contractures limit how far joints can move, and may make transfers difficult and bracing for walking almost impossible. Joints that commonly get stuck due to muscle contractures include hips, knees, and ankles. The next section describes a sample stretching program that addresses these potential problem spots.

SAMPLE STRETCHING PROGRAM

Perform each of the following stretches three to five times. Hold each stretch 10 to 30 seconds. Stretch muscles firmly and gently. DO NOT bounce. You may feel some discomfort while stretching, but you should never feel pain.

1. Hamstring Stretch: Sit on a mat with your legs straight out in front of you. Keeping your back straight, slowly lean forward. You may feel an uncomfortable stretch at the back of your legs.

2. Heel Cord Stretch: Still sitting with your legs straight out in front of you, grasp your feet with your hands or with a towel. Keeping your knees straight, pull your feet toward you. You may feel a stretch at the back of your legs below the knee.

3. Low Back Stretch: Lie on your back. Use both arms to slowly raise your knees to your chest.

4. Hip Flexor Stretch: Lie on your stomach with your legs straight out behind you. Bend one knee and grasp the leg above the ankle, pulling it towards your buttocks. Repeat on each leg.

5. Corner Stretch: Sitting in your wheelchair or standing in a doorway, place your hands on each side of the door frame behind you at ear level. Lean forward. You should feel a stretch across your chest.

6. Shoulder Stretch: Grasp one arm behind your head at the elbow. Pull the arm toward the opposite shoulder. You should feel a stretch at the back of your arm.

Aerobic Training

Aerobic exercise strengthens the heart and lungs and improves muscle endurance. Continuous activity that works lots of muscles and makes your heart beat faster is aerobic exercise. This means that while exercising, your heart needs to beat FAST for 20 to 45 minutes without resting. If you are between 13 and 21 years old, your heart needs to beat approximately 130 times per minute while performing aerobic activity.

The formula for determining your optimum heart rate is: 70% of (200 minus your age). That is, .70 x (200 - your age). For example, if you are 17, you would figure your optimum rate like this:

$$200 - 17 = 183$$
$$183 \times .7 = 128.1.$$

Your heart should beat about 128 times a minute during aerobic exercise.

A good rule of thumb is this: if you can't talk to a friend while exercising, then you're exercising too hard. At first, you may need to take one-minute rests, but if you faithfully exercise 3 to 5 days every week, you'll be surprised at how quickly you can go for 20 minutes without stopping.

Aerobic activity can be swimming, cycling, riding a stationary bicycle, walking, or running. If you use a wheelchair, your options include arm ergometry, rapid wheelchair propulsion, and wheelchair aerobics. Many wheelchair sports such as basketball, tennis, and track can also be aerobic exercise.

Arm Ergometry: An arm ergometer is a stationary bicycle that you pedal with your hands. For people who have the ability to use their arms and their legs, some models of ergometers can be pedaled with feet *or* with hands. If you need more variety than riding a stationary bike provides, some wheelchair companies offer a hand cycling attachment that can be put on your wheelchair to convert it to an all-terrain hand cycle!

Rapid Wheelchair Propulsion: Rapidly push your wheelchair around the neighborhood, around a track, or on a wheelchair treadmill.

You can get more information on arm ergometers, hand cycle attachments, and wheelchair treadmills by contacting a local medical supplier or wheelchair vendor.

Wheelchair Aerobics: There are many, many aerobic tapes for people with physical disabilities and for wheelchair users. You can order the following videotapes from a local bookstore or video store:

- Richard Simmons' *Reach For Fitness:*
  Special Exercises for the Physically Challenged
  Karl Lorimar Home Video
- *Wheelercise*
  Maura Productions, Inc.

You can also order the following video directly:

- *Keep Fit While You Sit*
  Slabo Productions
  Alexander Slabo
  1057 South Crescent Heights Blvd.
  Los Angeles, CA 90035
  Phone: 213-935-8624

Finally, for a current list of aerobic videos for people with physical dissabilities and wheelchair users, called the Paralyzed Veterans of America at 602-224-0500.

Wheelchair Sports

Are you interested in sports? Having spina bifida and using a wheelchair doesn't mean you can't be a competitive athlete. Many people who use wheelchairs play basketball, cycle, play tennis, and participate in track and field events. You can learn to ski . . . or earn a black belt in karate. Your choices are endless! So choose a sport and DO IT!

Call or write one of the following wheelchair sports organizations to find out how to contact your local wheelchair sports chapter.

Disabled Sports USA (formerly National Handicapped Sports)
451 Hungerford Drive, Suite 100
Rockville, MD 20850
Phone: 301-217-0960

Wheelchair Sports USA
(formerly National Wheelchair Athletic Association)
3595 East Fountain Boulevard, Suite L-1
Colorado Springs, CO 80910
719-574-1150

Special Olympics International (SOI)
1350 New York Avenue, NW
Suite 500
Washington, DC 20005
Phone: 202-628-3630

Wheelchair sports are like other aerobic exercises. Before you practice or participate in an event, you need to warm up your muscles with light activity. After exercise, cool down and stretch. Although you *can* substitute many wheelchair sports for your aerobic exercise routine, you *can't* necessarily substitute other events such as shotput for a strengthening or weight training routine.

Weight Training

Weight training increases the strength of specific muscle groups. Where aerobic training uses lots of muscles, weight training uses only a few muscles. Aerobic training increases endurance, or *how long* muscles can go, while weight training increases strength, or *how much* muscles can lift.

It can be very important to strengthen your muscles, particularly your triceps and shoulder muscles. To transfer by yourself in and out of your wheelchair and to use a walker, crutches, or a wheelchair efficiently, you need strength above and beyond that of your friends without spina bifida to keep up.

More is not necessarily better. Lifting too much weight can hurt growing bones. When growing bone is hurt, it may stop growing. This can lead to unequal limb lengths and back pain. Lifting weights too often can cause overuse injuries. Performing a 20- to 30-minute weight program 2 to 3 times each week is all that you need to increase muscle strength. Muscle soreness a day or two after weight training is normal. Give sore muscles time to recover; never lift weights two days in a row.

FINDING AN ACCESSIBLE GYM

Fitness centers are legally required to make their buildings accessible to wheelchair users under Title III of the Americans with Disabilities Act (ADA). At the time of this writing, however, they are *not* required to provide wheelchair accessible weight training equipment.

Adaptive weight training equipment does exist and can be purchased through a variety of manufacturers. Information on equipment and manufacturers can be found in the resources listed at the end of this chapter. If you want additional and up-to-date information on the legal responsibility of fitness centers to provide adaptive weight equipment, call the ADA Information Line at the U.S. Department of Justice (1-800-514-0301).

Unfortunately, very few gyms have weight training programs designed for individuals with disabilities. This means looking for a gym can be a challenge. Don't pay for membership to a gym until you call, and, most importantly, visit several local exercise and physical fitness centers. Ask if the facility has wheelchair accessible weight equipment. Ask if they have dumbbells or wrap weights. If they do, try it out! Most centers offer a free visit before asking you to pay for a membership. Fortunately, successful weight training does not depend on the use of expensive weight machines. You can create an excellent strengthening program using dumbbells or wrap weights.

SAMPLE UPPER EXTREMITY STRENGTHENING PROGRAM

Three times a week, perform each of the following exercises in one to three sets of ten repetitions. It's very important for your safety to use a buddy, or weight lifting partner, each time you do the exercises. This is especially true if you are using barbells. Without a partner to spot you, your muscles may become over-tired, causing you to drop the weights and injure yourself. Your program should take only 20 to 30 minutes.

IMPORTANT: With a physical therapist or weight lifting instructor, determine how much weight you should lift and review good form. Breathe out while you lift; breathe in as you return to starting position. When you can do one set of ten repetitions easily, increase the weight by one to three pounds.

1. Overhead Press: Grasp dumbbells at shoulder level with palms facing forward. Lift dumbbells overhead until your elbows are straight and the dumbbells are above your shoulders. Slowly return to starting position.

2. Upright Rows: Hold dumbbells close together on your lap with your elbows straight and palms down. Lift them in a rowing motion to your chest with your elbows pointed toward the ceiling. Slowly return to starting position.

3. Wheelchair Pushups: Grab your armrests. Push your body up out of your seat until your elbows are straight. Slowly lower your body back into your seat.

4. Shoulder Abduction: Hold dumbbell at your side with your palm facing forward. Lift your arm straight out to the side and over your head. Slowly return to starting position. Repeat on other arm.

5. Shoulder Flexion: Hold dumbbell at your side with your palm facing toward your body. Lift your arm straight out in front of you and over your head. Slowly return to starting position. Repeat on other arm.

6. Triceps Curls: Hold dumbbell behind your neck with your elbow pointing toward the ceiling. Straighten your elbow, raising your hand toward the ceiling. Slowly return to starting position.

 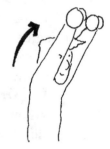

7. Biceps Curls: Grasp dumbbell at your side with your palm facing forward. Bend your elbow, lifting dumbbell toward your shoulder. Slowly return to starting position. Repeat on other arm.

What Next?

Now you have the know-how to create your own unique fitness program. But, where do you start? Stretching, strengthening, and aerobic exercise are ALL important: **stretching** for preventing contractures; **strengthening** for improving transfer ability and efficiency of wheelchair propulsion or walking with an assistive device; and **aerobic exercise** for strengthening the heart and lungs and improving overall muscle endurance. A complete fitness program should include all three kinds of exercise.

Remember, you need to perform aerobic exercise three to five times a week, but strengthening exercise only two to three times a week to see results. So, for example, you may want to do aerobic exercise on Mondays, Wednesdays, and Fridays and lift weights on Tuesdays and Thursdays. You may want to lift weights on Saturdays, too. Whether you do aerobic or strengthening exercise, make sure you warm up with light activity before and cool down with stretches afterward. This way, every time you exercise, you stretch, too.

What exercises do you plan to do? Twenty minutes of wheelchair laps? An aerobic tape? *When* do you plan to do it? Before school? During the week? *Where* will you do it? *How* will you get there? WRITE IT DOWN! Then, before you start anything, talk to your doctor.

1. **STRETCH** out those tight spots!
2. **Improve your endurance** and *go*, GO, **GO** with aerobic exercise!
3. **STRENGTHEN** your muscles, *and . . .*
4. **SHOW 'EM** your stuff with wheelchair sports!

With proper exercise, you will have the tools it takes to KEEP UP, KEEP FIT, and KEEP GOING!

Resources

Conditioning with Physical Disabilities. Keith F. Lockette and Ann M. Keyes. Champaign, IL: Human Kinetics (P.O. Box 5076, Champaign, IL 61825-5076. 800-747-4457), 1994.

A practical book with beautiful illustrations and simple descriptions of all types of exercise.

Sports and Recreation for the Disabled. Michael J. Paciorek and Jeffrey A. Jones. Carmel, IN: Cooper Publishing Group (701 Congressional Blvd., #340, Carmel, IN 46032), 1994.

A resource book with lists of adaptive equipment, wheelchair sports organizations, etc.

Sports 'n Spokes. Paralyzed Veterans of America. 2111 East Highland Ave., Suite 180, Phoenix, AZ 85016. 602-224-0500.

A magazine devoted to wheelchair sports and recreation.

Contributors

Linda Custis-Allen, M.S., OTR/L, is an occupational therapist with over 20 years professional experience in the areas of physical dysfunction and developmental disorders. She has participated as a member of the Cincinnati Center for Developmental Disorders Myelomeningocele Team for over five years. In this role, she has provided ADL (activities of daily living) and equipment evaluations, including wheelchair assessments, provided developmental assessment information, and written parent education materials.

Roberta Hills, R.N., M.S., is a clinical nurse specialist who has specialized in the care and needs of children with chronic handicapping conditions. For nearly twenty years, she assisted families and children in management of their toileting programs. In addition, she has provided assistance to schools on the toileting and learning problems of children with disabilities. She started a research program focused specifically on ways to help children with spina bifida become independent in bowel self-care.

Catherine Lowe, M.S., P.T., graduated in December 1989, from the University of Indianapolis with a Master of Science in physical therapy. She has been a staff therapist at Children's Hospital Medical Center and has served the Cincinnati Center for Developmental Myelomeningocele Clinic since March 1990. She has participated in wheelchair evaluations and ambulation and mobility training, and has provided physical therapy services for clients with developmental disorders.

Marlene Lutkenhoff, R.N., M.S.N., is a clinical nurse specialist in the field of parent/child nursing. She is the service coordinator for the Myelomeningocele (Spina Bifida) Clinic at University Affiliated Cincinnati Center for Developmental Disorders. As service coordinator, she monitors a child's progress from birth to age 21. She is responsible for writing family care plans and helping the family find the services and support they need. Her job responsibilities include teaching families and community agencies, particularly schools, about Myelomeningocele.

Sonya G. Oppenheimer, M.D., is a developmental pediatrican and Director of the Department of Pediatrics at the Cincinnati Center for Developmental Disorders. She is Professor of Pediatrics at the University of Cincinnati. Dr. Oppenheimer has been the Director of the Spina Bifida Clinic since 1971.

Sharon Sellet has a B.S. in Art Education from the University of Cincinnati and is the parent of a teenager with spina bifida. She is a former art teacher and has served as Parent Coordinator for the Family/Professional Resource Center since the program began in 1991. Sharon assists parents of children with chronic conditions and disabilities and professionals working with these children in finding resources and support in meeting their needs in the community.

Nan Tobias, M.S.N., R.N., CS, P.N.P., is a urologic nurse practitioner. For seven years, she has worked with a variety of children's problems, ranging from enuresis to neurogenic bladder.

Artist

Eric Lutkenhoff has won many art awards, including a scholarship to the College of Mount St. Joseph in Cincinnati, Ohio, where he is continuing to develop his skills in the artistic field.

Index

Abdomen, 72, 73, 78
Access, 99, 102, 128.
  See also Wheelchairs
"Access Amtrak," 53
"Access Travel: Airports," 53
Accommodations.
  See Adaptations
Accountant, 18
Activities of daily living (ADLs),
  11-19
ADA, 10, 100, 101, 108, 128
Adaptations, 52, 82, 90, 101, 102
  health and, 116, 119-20, 128
Adaptogs, 14
Advocacy, 82, 100
Aerobic training, 125-26
Agencies, 106-108
Alcohol, 118-19
Allergies, 9-10, 77
Alveeno, 22
Ambulator, 43-44
Americans with Disabilities Act
  (ADA), 10, 100, 101, 108, 128
Anatomy, 71
Ankle foot orthoses (AFO's), 45
Ankles, 8
Anti-crouch AFO's, 45
Anus, 27-28, 29, 32
Appreciation, 67
Architect, 19
Arms, 6

Arnold Chiari, 6
Assignment book, 87
Attention, 81, 85-86, 88
Attitude, 12, 58
Attractiveness, 73
Automatic teller machine (ATM), 98
Aviano U.S.A., 14
Back, 3, 5, 6, 8
Backbone, 3, 8, 119
Balance, 8, 52
Balls, 120
Basis, 22
Bathing, 13, 23
Bath lift, hydraulic, 18
Bath mats, nonskid, 18
Benadryl™, 23
Big Brothers, 108
Big Sisters, 108
Biking, 116
Birth control pills, 77
Birth defect, 4
Bladder, 4, 5, 6, 7, 23
  accidents, 75, 76
  care, 35-37, 39, 74, 96
Blood, 5
Blood pressure, 7
Body systems, 5
Bones, 5, 8-9
Bowel, 4, 5, 6, 7
  accidents, 75, 76
  care of, 27-33, 38, 96

Boy Scouts, 108
Braces, 3, 8, 9, 14, 45-46
Brain, 3, 5-7
Brainstorm, 88
Breast exam, 120
Breathing, 6, 8, 119
Brothers, 63-69, 98
Bureau of Motor Vehicles, 51-52
Burns, 23
Bus lines, 53, 97
Calcium alginate, 24
Calendar, 87
Calories, 116-18
Camp, 96
Cancer, 72-73
Career planning, 95-109
Carpenter, 19
Car rentals, 53
Casters, 50
Catheter, 7, 12, 39
Catheterization, 90
Causes, of spina bifida, 4
Cellular phone, 120
Cerebral-spinal fluid, 5, 6
Cervical tissue, 72-73
Cervix, 73, 77
Cesarean section (C-section), 78
Charts, 84, 89
Choir, 96
Church, 108
Cleansing, 24

Clubs, 96
College, 90, 101, 102
Colleges with Programs for Students with Learning Disabilities, 102
Colon, 27-28, 31
Commode chair, 18
Community ambulator, 43
Constipation, 28, 30
Consumer Information Center, 108
Contractor, 19, 45-46
Contractures, 9, 50
Cornell Notetaking System, 89
Counselor, 102, 104
Cramps, 72
Creams, 22
Cross frames, 49
Crutches, 8, 44-45, 124
CT scan, 7
Cushions, 51
Dating, 73-74
Debridement, 24-25
Decision-making, 97
Definition, of spina bifida, 3, 4
Degenerative joint disease, 9
Dental care, 120
Dentist, 120
Department of Justice, 128
Depression, 115
Depro Provera®, 77
Diagrams, 89
Diaphragm, 77
Diarrhea, 28
Diets, 25
Digital stimulation, 7, 32
Disabled Sports USA, 126
Discrimination, 100
Diseases, sexually transmitted, 77
Ditropan™, 23, 30, 39, 119
Doctor, 6, 9, 71, 75-78, 86, 118
Double vision, 5
Dressing, 13-16
Dressing sticks, 16
Drinks, 37-38
Driver's Education, 51
Driving, 51-52, 98, 120
Drugs, 118-19
Dysphagia, 6
Eating, 23, 25, 115-18.
    See also Food
Education, 12, 13, 40-41, 48, 99
Egg, 76
Ejaculation, 75, 77

Emotions, 66-67, 113-16
Employment, 48, 90, 96, 98-101, 108
Enemas, 7, 32, 33
Engineer, 52
Equal Employment Opportunity Commission (EEOC), 101
Equipment, 18, 48, 52, 58, 116
    dressing, 15-16
    medical, 12-13
    transfer, 17
Erection, 75
Etiology, 4
Exercise, 8, 9, 31, 124-31
Family, 63-69
Fatigue, 5
Federal Help for Individuals with Disabilities, 108
Federation for Children with Special Needs, 91
Feeling, 8, 9, 29, 50, 75, 78
Feelings, 66-67, 113-16
Feet, 8
Fertility, 76-77
Fine motor skills, 88
Fire department, 120
Fire extinguishers, 120
Fitness, 8, 124-31
Flexibility, 124-25
Focus, 81, 85-86, 88
Folic acid, 4, 78
Food, 30, 31, 37. *See also* Eating
Forearm crutches, 44
4-H Club, 108
Fractures, 8-9
Frames, wheelchair, 49
Friends, 40-41, 57-62
Gas, 74
Genetic counselors, 77
Genetics, 4, 77
Genitals, 72-77
Girl Scouts, 108
Gloves, 9, 32, 73
Goals, 82, 99
Goodwill Industries, 106
Grab bars, 17, 18
Gratitude, 67
Growth, 5, 8
Guidance counselor, 102, 104
Gyms, 128
Gynecologist, 72
Headaches, 5

Health, 108, 113-22
Heat, 9
HEATH Resource Center, 91
Hen's Nest, 14
Hip knee ankle foot orthoses (HKAFO's), 45-46
Hips, 8
Hobbies, 102
Homework, 85
Household ambulator, 43
Hydraulic bath lift, 18
Hydrocephalus, 4, 5, 6
Hydrocolloid, 24
Hydrogel, 24
Hydromyelia, 6
Hypertonic dressing, 24
Incidence, 4
Incontinence, 35
Independence, 57-62, 97, 108
Individualized Education Program (IEP), 13, 40, 90, 98-100
Individuals with Disabilities Education Act (IDEA), 90
Information, recall of, 81, 82
Insurance, 13, 48, 98, 103, 121
Internal Revenue Service (IRS), 18-19, 47
Interviews, 100
Irritability, 5
Jewish Vocational Services, 106-107
Jobs, 48, 90, 96, 98-99, 102-104, 106
Joints, 5, 8-9
Karl Lorimar Home Video, 126
Keep Fit While You Sit, 126
Keyboarding, 82, 96
Kidneys, 7, 35-39, 75.
    See also Urinary system
Kissing, 74
Knee ankle foot orthoses (KAFO's), 45
K-Y Jelly, 32, 72, 76
Labor, 78
Lab tests, 6
Language, 88
Latex, 9-10, 73, 77
Laurel Designs, 14
Lawyer Referral and Information Services, 100, 101
Lawyers, 100, 101

Laxatives, 32
Learning, 81-93
Legal Aid Society, 100, 101
Legs, 4, 8
Lesion, location of, 8
Levsin™, 39
Library, 71, 98
Lifts, 17
Liquids, 37-38
Lists, 84
Long-handled sponges, 18
Long leg braces, 45-46
Love, 74
Lubricants, 22, 75-76
Lubrifax, 32
Lungs, 8. See also Breathing
Magnetic resonance imaging
    (MRI), 6, 7
"Mapping," 84
Maura Productions, Inc., 126
Meals, 30, 31.
    See also Eating; Food
Medical care, 120-22
Medical supplies, 40
Medicine, 9, 30, 31, 39, 86, 115
Memory, 81, 82-85, 88
Menstrual cycle, 76
Menstruation, 72, 76
Mental Health Services, 115
Mitrofanoff, 39
Mnemonics, 85
Mobility, 3-4, 6, 8, 43-54, 86,
    97-98
Modifications. See Adaptations
Money, 13, 98
Movement, 3, 6, 8, 22
Muscles, 3, 9, 72
Music, 96
Myelomeningocele, 4
Nadeau, Kathleen G., 102
National Council on Independent
    Living, 107
National Information Center for
    Children & Youth with
    Disabilities, 91
National Spina Bifida
    Association, 115
National Wheelchair Athletic
Association, 127
Neck, 6
Nerves, 3, 8, 28, 29, 36, 72
Nervous system, 5, 81-82

Neurosurgeon, 5, 6
Neutrogena, 22
Newspapers, 103
Nonskid bath mats, 18
Notetaking, 88-89
Nurse, 12, 19, 71
Nutrition, 23, 116-18.
    See also Food
Obstetrician, 76, 78
Occupational therapist (OT), 12,
    19, 48, 90
Operations, 5, 6, 8, 9, 24
    mobility, 48, 64
    urinary tract, 39
Organization, 82, 84, 86-87,
    106-108
Orgasm, 75
Orthopedic system, 5
Ovaries, 73
Ovulation, 76
Pads, 40, 72
Pain, 9
Pap smear, 72-73, 120
Paralysis, 3
Parents, 71
Parent Training & Information
    Centers, 91
Parks, 116
Pee, 7, 23, 35-38
Pelvic exam, 72-73, 120
Penis, 71, 74-77
Period, 72
Peristalsis, 28
Pharmacy, 12
Physical therapist (PT), 8, 12,
    19, 48, 90
Pills, birth control, 77
Planner, 87
Planning, 60-61, 87, 95-109
Plastic, 10
Pneumatic wheels, 50
Police department, 120
Positions, sexual, 75
Practice, 13
Pregnancy, 72, 76-78
Pressure relief cushion, 23
Pressure sores, 21-22, 51, 124
Privacy, 72
Probanthine™, 23, 39
Problem solving, 60-61, 86
Proofreading, 89
Publication 502, 19

Question, 84
Raised toilet seat, 18
Ramps, 17, 120
Range of motion, 51
Reach For Fitness: Special
    Exercises for the Physically
    Challenged, 126
Reaching devices, 15
Read, 84
Reasons, for spina bifida, 4
Recall, 81, 82
Recite, 84
Recording for the Blind &
    Dyslexic, 92
Recreation, 116
Rectum, 27-28
Redness, of skin, 9
Rehabilitation services, 106
Related services, 90
Relationships, 57-62
Renal scan, 38
Renal ultrasound, 38
Reproductive organs, 71-77
Resource room, 90
Resources, 13
Respect, 65-66, 72
Respiration, 6, 8
Rest, 9
Resume, 103, 104
Review, 84
Rights, 99-101
Rigid frames, 49
ROHO cushion, 51
Routine, 87
Rubber, 9
Safety, 119-20
SAT Services for Students with
    Disabilities, 90, 91
Scar tissue, 5, 6
School, 12, 13, 40-41, 48, 99
Science fair, 96
Scoliosis, 6, 8, 50, 119
Seats, 50-51
Section 504 plan, 40, 98-100, 102
Seizures, 4
Self-care, 11-19, 96
Semen, 77
Sensation, 8, 9, 29, 50, 75, 78
Sexual intercourse, 74-76
Sexuality, 71-78
Sexually transmitted diseases, 77
Shields, 40

Shoe horn, 15
Shorthand, 89
Short leg braces, 45
Shower seat, 18
Shower wheelchair, 18
Shunt, 4, 5, 6
Siblings, 63-69, 98
Silicone, 10
Simmons, Richard, 126
Sisters, 63-69, 98
Sitting, 8
Skin, 3, 21-25
Slabo Productions, 126
Sleep, 115
Smoke detectors, 120
Smoking, 118-19
Soap, 22, 24
Social Security Income (SSI), 103
Social skills, 59-62
Sock donners, 15
Soiling, 75, 76
Solid wheels, 50
Sores, pressure, 21-22, 51, 124
Special Clothes, 15
Special education, 90
Special Olympics International
   (SOI), 127
Sperm, 72, 75
Sphincter, 28, 29
Spina bifida
   causes of, 4
   definition of, 3, 4
   effects on fertility, 76-77
   effects on learning, 81-93
   effects on movement, 3, 6, 8
   having a baby with, 77
   occurrence rate, 4
   surgery for, 5, 6, 8, 9, 24
Spina Bifida Association of
   America, 10, 69, 92, 108
Spinal cord, 3, 5, 7, 36
Spinal fluid, 5, 6
Spine, 3, 5-7
Spokes, 84
Sponge, long-handled, 18
Sports, 96, 116, 126-27
Steps, 17
Stomach, 5
Stool, 27-28, 31, 32
Strategies, classroom, 81-93
Strength, 51, 128-31
Stretching, 124-25, 130-31

Subway, 97
Sun screen lotion, 23
Suppositories, 7, 32
Surgery, 5, 6, 8, 9, 24
   mobility and, 48, 64
   urinary tract, 39
Survey, 84
Survival Guide for College
   Students with ADD or LD, 102
Swallowing, 6
Swelling, 9
Syringomyelia, 6
Tampons, 72
Taxes, 18, 98
Taxi cabs, 97
Teachers, 57
Technical training, 101
Techniques, for learning, 81-93
Testicles, 120
Tests, 6, 90
Tethered cord, 5-6
Therapeutic ambulator, 44
Thinking, 88
Time management, 82
Tiredness, 5
Title III, 128
"To Do" list, 87
Tofranil™, 23
Toileting, 35
Toilet seat, raised, 18
Tools, 81-93
Transfer bench, 18
Transfer boards, 17
Transfers, 8, 16-17, 22, 51
Transition plan, 52, 90, 98-100
Transparent film, 24
Transportation, 48, 52-53, 97,
   99-100, 104
Travel, 52-53
Treatment, 24-25
Trunk hip knee ankle foot
   orthoses (THKAFO's), 46
Tub bench, 13
Tutoring, 90
Typewriter, 90
United Cerebral Palsy
   Associations (UCPA), 107
United States Department of
   Education, 92
United States Government, 47
Ureters, 35, 36
Urethra, 35, 36, 37, 39

Urinary system, 5, 35-42, 75.
   See also Kidneys
Urinary tract infections, 35, 37-38
Urine, 7, 23, 35-38
Urodynamics, 39
Urologist, 38, 75
Uterus, 72, 73, 77, 78
Vacation planning, 52-53
Vagina, 71-75, 77
Valproic Acid, 4
Velcro, 14
Vesicoureteral reflux, 37, 38
Vinyl, 10, 32
Vision, 5, 51
Visual perceptual problems, 52
Visuals, 89
Vitamin B, 4, 78
Vitamin C, 25
Vitamin supplements, 4, 25, 78
Vocational rehabilitation, 52, 106
Vocational training, 99, 101-102
Voiding Cystourethrogram
   (VCUG), 38
Volunteering, 96, 99, 103, 104
Vomiting, 5
Walkers, 8, 44-45, 52, 124
Walking, 3, 4, 6, 8, 9, 43-54
Warming up, 8-9
Washing, 22
Water, 23, 30, 37, 116
Weight, 117
Weight training, 128-31
Wet dreams, 72
Wetting, 75, 76
Wheelchairs, 3, 8, 14, 16.
   See also Access
   contractures and, 9
   health and, 116-118, 124-26
   mobility and, 44, 46-51, 52
   shower, 18
   sports, 126-27
Wheelchair Sports USA, 127
Wheelercise, 126
Wheelies Bentwear, 15
Wheels, 49-50, 84
White Pages, 47, 100, 101
Word processor, 90
Work, 48, 90, 96, 98-101, 108
Writing, 88-90
X-rays, 6, 7, 9, 38, 120
Yellow Pages, 51, 97, 100, 101, 115
Zinc, 25